THE GREAT PLAN

As Told

By

THE HOLY SPIRIT

To

Wendy and Jillian
Earth Angels

Written by

Gwen Michalek

Illustrated & Edited by

Jill Emerson

<u>Other Books:</u>

"Earth Angels" (Available on Amazon and Kindle)

<u>The Little Book Series</u>

(Available to listen to and download in pdf for free on our Website/You-tube Channel.)

#1 She Who Was Afraid

#2 Is Anybody in There

#3 The Soul Train

#4 When Heaven Can't Wait

#5 The Truth Revealed

#6 The Soul Catcher

#7 An Angel Named Honey

#8 The Soul Survivor

#9 The Spiritual Warrior

#10 Going Home

#11 The Purpose of Life

THE GREAT PLAN

www.earthangelsbook.com

Email: earthangelsbook@gmail.com

Contents

Part 3

Part 4

THE GREAT PLAN

DEDICATION

This book is dedicated to the Holy Spirit! As Earth Angels, Wendy and Jillian have been Divinely inspired to write **"The Great Plan'**, guided by The Holy Spirit. As a result, this book is dedicated to our friend and counselor, the Holy Spirit, without whom it would have been impossible to write.

The Father's Great Plan has been shared so all will understand that which is the reality. Not a reality based on Man's interpretation, but one that removed the veil so all can fully grasp the essence of life.

We pray all will come to know and love the Holy Spirit as we do. For truly, there can be no other relationship to compare with the loving Spirit of our Lord and Savior, Jesus Christ.

May the Lord Bless and keep you all,

Wendy and Jillian

ACKNOWLEDGEMENT

Jillian and I would like to express our heartfelt thanks to those who, over the years, have supported ABBA and Company. It has been a journey like none other on earth.

While there are many Earth Angels scattered throughout the World, we would like to give a special thanks to Brenda who we affectionately refer to as "Sunshine". A name which is representative of her smile, and that captivates the heart of all who cross her path. Her enthusiastic support, over the years, has been a gift from the Father. She is truly an Earth Angel.

Thank you to our guys, Dick and Tom whom without their patience and support, "The Great Plan" would never have been accomplished, in a timely manner. Your support over the years has been invaluable and a blessing.

I, Wendy, love you Dick with all my heart as you truly have been and continue to be the "Wind beneath my wings".

THE GREAT PLAN

And most of all thank you Jesus for sending the Holy Spirit to assist us in writing "The Great Plan".

Love,

Wendy & Jillian

INTRODUCTION

Have you ever wondered why you seem to know something others do not? Have you ever felt as though you do not fit in? It is not that you consider yourself special, if anything, the feeling was quite opposite. Yet, for the most part, you never felt threatened or unloved as you had a natural love of Jesus and had always felt His immense love for you. It always seemed strange that there were so many who did not seem to know Him as you do. Even stranger were the ones who went to church every Sunday, but never talked about Jesus or mentioned His name outside of church. As you became older, you realized, more than ever, you were not the norm, but rather the exception.

If you have happened to come upon this book, it is not by accident. You, like many other souls who inhabit the earth in these times, are an integral part of our Father's plan. As a matter of fact, you have chosen to participate in what is about to unfold before your very eyes. That is right. You chose to participate in the **Greatest Plan** of all time.

THE GREAT PLAN

Although your mission may not be the exact same as another, rest assured, you have within all you need to fulfill your destiny!

PROLOGUE

THE GLORY,

Mine eyes have seen the glory of the coming of the Lord. Those who have eyes to see will see what lies ahead as well as what is in store for all who stand strong against the forces of evil upon the earth. This is not a strength which comes from the physical, but rather, that which is of our Father's Heavenly Spirit. Those who will stand strong in the times of trial know they are created in their Father's image, and as such, are empowered with all that is of His Spirit

Jesus exclaimed to His beloved disciples *"It is far better that I leave so another can take My place."* The same Spirit who resides in Jesus and the Heavenly Father resides in all who acknowledge this reality. A reality that empowers God's precious souls with all that is of the Father. For every soul is created in the Father's image.

In these times of trial, many souls were being held hostage by that which was of the physical. As well as by that which they understood to be the sum-total of who they were, and of who they identified as "**self**".

Jesus had removed the veil of darkness to awaken man to what was the reality, hoping and praying, that in times of distress they would look to Him for the answers they were seeking. He hoped they would have opened their eyes to what they once thought was right and true to satisfy the longing which came from within.

There would be a hunger the world could not satisfy. More and more acts of violence were now appearing on the world stage, as nation turned against nation, while at the same time, rumors of war were no longer a rumor but an ever-increasing reality.

The hearts of many had grown cold, portraying an aura of indifference, which once was described as complacency. Webster defines complacency as: *a feeling of satisfaction with oneself disregarding that which does not directly affect one's own being.* Indifference on the other hand, shows lack of concern, importance, or sympathy. In short, lack of Interest.

This uncaring lackadaisical attitude would now greatly contribute to the fall of mankind. This attitude would open the door for the Antichrist to appear on the world stage. For man had lost his ability to discern the difference between right and wrong, seeking only satisfaction for his temporal needs. Yes, all that would attend to his worldly needs leaving little if no room for that which was of the spiritual.

"Oh", thought Wendy and Jillian, "if only more had understood the meaning of the times. If only more had paid attention to that which was transpiring throughout the world. One nation under God was no longer united in the United States. The United States no longer adhered to the Godly principles it was originally founded upon."

These were the times which had been foretold in the Book of Revelation. Times that were rapidly heading towards what had been referred to as the tribulation. While the Lord's mercy has kept the tribulation at bay, Wendy and Jillian knew, without a shadow of a doubt that man was now approaching a precipice upon which way he turned would not only decide his personal fate, but the fate of the world overall.

Currently, there are those on earth who were participating in what was known as the *Extreme Plan* and believed themselves to be a race far superior to the common man. As such, they held no affinity to God or those Commandments which would support the belief that all men were created equal. The political arena had become a hotbed of hatred, division, and public unrest. It became a weapon used by Satan to distract, deter and divide. In essence, to keep mankind chained to that which would direct man's eyes to self and selfish interests. One would no longer take responsibility for how he responded to his fellow man. In many ways, much of the world has become a dog-eat-dog society.

We have given you, the reader, a general idea of how the world was being viewed by our Heavenly Father. Jesus knew there would be far too many souls who would be subjected to a myriad of horrific events that the enemy had prepared for this precise moment in time.

Wendy and Jillian had recently completed **The Great Plan** which they had been chosen to write through the promptings of the Holy Spirit. A book, that for many, would reveal that which was the reality. Not that which was based on religion, but rather one that would act as a tonic for man's soul. A tonic that would open man's eyes to what was not an illusion, but one that explained the reality of not only who they truly are, but what they are capable of as a spiritual being.

Upon reading **The *Great Plan*,** the Father hoped one would understand not only the meaning of the times but the choice they soon would be called to make. A choice of which there could be no turning back from. This choice would affect not only the conditions one found themselves in, but rather that which would enable one to participate in the *New World,* which was sure to come as our Father's Kingdom would soon reign on earth as it is in heaven.

This *New World* would demonstrate God's inherent Glory. A world that displays the beauty and grandeur of God's nature. It is a world like nothing the earth has seen before. Our Father's glory will be ever present within every believer who inhabits this *New World.* A world that supersedes what was once part and parcel of man's behavior.

All who reside in this *New World* are one with our Father's Spirit. For as it is in Heaven, let it therefore be on earth. Peace and harmony prevail as all live in accordance to the will of Jesus. That which exemplifies the mind of Christ is ever present in the *New World* that has now been established upon the earth. Hallelujah!

PART 1

CHAPTER 1
THE BEGINNING

It is difficult to know where to start as there was much that had transpired since Wendy and Jillian had been sent to earth in their newly assigned role of what would come to be known as **Earth Angels**. This assignment began in the heavens above long before their arrival on earth. For you see, Earth Angels were among those who would inhabit the earth prior to the return of Jesus who would eventually, along with His remnant church, reign on earth.

While it may seem as though what is about to be written in the following pages is far-fetched or even difficult to believe, it is a part of our *Father's Great Plan*. A plan that would come to be referred to as **"The Greatest Plan on Earth"**.

It is important to understand Heaven is a place much the same as Earth is a place. In both cases, each place is a reality and truly does exist. And so it is, that Jesus resides over Heaven, and suffice it so say, Lucifer/ Satan resides on Earth.

THE GREAT PLAN

Jesus' plan is a plan, that in the end, will destroy Satan and his legion of fallen angels once and for all. This plan would need to be precise and every detail would need to be tended to. Timing would be of the utmost importance. For this reason, much would need to transpire before the final battle would take place.

Jesus reigns in Heaven, along with His many angels who serve our Father with such immense dedication, embracing His will above all else. Mankind has a difficult time accepting or believing in that which he cannot see, yet there will be those on earth who will be given the spiritual ears and eyes in which to see and hear what mortal man does not.

Of course, this ability would play an integral role prior to Jesus' return to earth. For these are the souls who will help prepare the way for Jesus' Kingdom to reign on earth as it is in heaven.

This battle would end in the destruction of Lucifer and his fallen angels. St. Michael and his Heavenly Army had been fighting against them since the beginning of time. Soon, very soon, as Jesus' plan begins to unfold there will be those who inhabit the earth who will join forces with this majestic army forming the Supreme Army of which many, such as yourself, would play an integral role.

THE GREAT PLAN

CHAPTER 2
THE PREPARATION

Wendy and Jillian were to be among the many souls who would help prepare the way for our Father's Kingdom to reign on earth. You must understand, the Lord's time clock is not the same as mortal mans. What can seem like a brief span of time in eternal time, for mankind, could seem to be a great deal longer on earth.

As a result, there would be a span of time before the souls who inhabited the earth would understand from where they had come and where they would indeed return. And so, it would be for every soul who resided on earth, a period in which they would perfect those attributes that would be required in the final battle between good and evil.

Every soul would be endowed with a **Spiritual Gift** that would prove to be the exact weapon one would need in order to accomplish the specific mission they were assigned. These gifts would become the very weapons that would play a major role in defeating the enemy. These were weapons that man would generally not consider using in a battle, yet for a Spiritual Being they would far surpass any mortal weapon of which man could devise.

The **Gifts of the Spirit are**; *wisdom, knowledge, discerning of spirits, faith, miracles, healing, tongues, interpretation and prophecy.* These gifts could not be learned in the School of Life as they were given by the Father according to their purpose. That which each soul was destined to complete.

Every soul has a history which is recorded in the *Book of Life*. This history keeps a detailed record of the **Fruits of the Spirit** *(love, joy, peace, forbearance, kindness, gentleness, goodness, faithfulness and self-control)* that each soul has become proficient in and those that need perfecting. Every teaching includes the precise lesson that will enable the soul to cultivate the very ideals of our Heavenly Father. Therefore, they cannot be earned they must be learned. The history of each soul reflects those ideals or fruits they are most proficient in and those which they are not. Each soul, as a result, has a DNA which includes the fruit or fruits he has already mastered.

CHAPTER 3
THE SCHOOL OF LIFE

Up until this moment of time, there has always been a School of Life that the soul could attend on earth. No soul was ever forced to attend, yet, most souls desired to do so. For the School of Life on earth provided an excellent opportunity for each soul to advance in his studies. An opportunity that would enable one to become more proficient in what some would refer to as the *Fruits of The Spirit*. The ultimate goal was to become more fully enlightened in the ways of our Heavenly Father.

Each soul would carefully consider the very conditions into which they would be born. While some of these conditions would seem less than desirable, they would, in fact, be the exact conditions that would enable the soul to master what it needed to learn.

In heaven all souls are endowed with free will much the same as humans are endowed with free will. Those who reside in heaven embrace the will of their Heavenly Father, which is not necessarily the case with those who inhabit the earth.

Free will, for much of mankind, would be responsible for the very choices he would make. Choices that would help to develop his own personal lesson plan. All lessons arise, therefore, from the choices which are made. Once a mistake had been acknowledged, the soul must then seek another lesson and make a higher choice as the opportunity arises.

Often, these choices would be viewed by mortal man as a mistake. Yet, it was through these so-called mistakes man was able to learn what his soul was desperately seeking. It is well known throughout our Father's Kingdom that Jesus does not view mistakes in the same manner as man does. For He knows *mistakes are an integral part of one's lesson plan. Lessons that once learned would enable one to share their newfound wisdom with those who cross their path.* These choices were influenced by the conditions one found themselves in. These choices were influenced by that which was of the exterior. The world is the way it is because of the choices man has made. These choices can make elements of life more difficult, yet one can choose whether to accept them or not. As a result, **humans approached life from the outside in,**

whereas the soul approached life from the inside out. Up until now the School of Life afforded an opportunity for this to transpire, yet in order for this to take place it was imperative the soul be able to connect with the Spirit. As a Spiritual Being, this connection was necessary for the soul to move forward with the mission he was longing to complete. It is at this point the soul understands the purpose of life is to *LEARN, TO SERVE AND TO GROW.*

Before the soul enrolls in the School of Life there are terms and conditions that would need to be agreed upon. One would say it is a contract drawn up between the Heavenly Father and the soul. This would be a covenant which could not be broken.

Life Conditions Contract:

1. The soul must understand that upon arriving to earth he would have no memory of from where he had come. This would ensure the soul would not be filled with an overwhelming desire to return home, no matter how difficult the lessons may become.

2. Every soul would be endowed with the gift of "free will" that would be responsible for the challenges the soul would face.

3. Each soul would choose the family they would be born into. A family that would provide the exact circumstances in which to learn what was necessary as a human being to accomplish their mission. Depending on what the soul was trying to achieve, some of these circumstances could seem less than desirable. Yet, they would provide the soul with the optimum opportunity to accomplish what their soul was trying to complete. Because these circumstances could present many difficult challenges for each soul, it was necessary they do not remember their prior existence in heaven. For when difficult times would arise, the desire to return home would overwhelm any desire the soul would have to remain on earth. Once the soul agreed to these conditions, he would then be ready to prepare for his earthly education.

<u>THE SCHOOL OF LIFE</u>

A wise old man once said to me,
no matter how hard you look
that which your soul is seeking
won't be found in any book.
The road your soul must travel
is the path that he must take.
It is a journey like none other
one that only he can make.
The School of Life on earth
is where the soul must surely go,
if he wants to master that of which
he truly needs to grow.
The choices he will make will form his lesson plan,
in hopes that in the end he will become a wiser man.
The wisdom he acquires will be
recorded in the Book of Life.
As he continues to master that which
would cause another strife.
For learn he must and learn he will
as he continues in his quest,
to draw closer to the mind of Christ
in hopes to pass the test.

THE GREAT PLAN

CHAPTER 4
THE SOUL

In order for the soul to take full benefit of everything the School of Life had to offer, it was important man understands the soul is the most important part of the human body. Your physical body, in which the soul resides, is merely a temporary residence that enables your soul to visit earth for a specific amount of time. In reality, you are a Citizen of Heaven. Heaven is where you are from and where you will return when your time on earth has ended. Your soul is history in the making, as your name is registered in our **Heavenly Father's Golden Book** that keeps a record of not only who you are but what has transpired over your eternal life. The definition of eternal is: *lasting or existing forever without end.* Humans define lifetime based on the duration of one's physical body. Much of mankind now believes that when the physical body no longer functions life then ceases to be.

Nothing could be farther from the truth. You are not the sum-total of your physical body, but rather a

14

great deal more than what most of mankind acknowledges to be true. Your physical body depends on the five senses (*sight, hearing, touch, smell and taste*) in order to function while on earth. Without these senses your physical self would cease to exist. As important as these senses are to the human condition, they do not attend to the needs of your soul. They do not tend to the needs of the most important part of who you are.

In reality, your soul can indeed exist without the human body, yet the human body cannot exist without the soul for it would serve no earthly purpose. You are a Spiritual Being and, as such, capable of far more than what man acknowledges.

Your soul understands who you truly are and the true purpose for your earthly existence. Much the same as the physical body relies on the five senses in order to exist on earth, your soul relies on a Divine sense (*a sense which man often refers to as the sixth sense*). This sense, when exercised, is manna for the soul as it enables the soul to communicate with his Heavenly Father. Yet, much of mankind does not pay attention to this sixth sense as the physical body does not require it to sustain itself. So, in-reality, man is equipped with six senses not five and is often not acknowledged as such.

This Divine sense provides the soul with a way and a means to communicate with His Heavenly Father. For in truth, what kind of a Father would send His beloved on a journey without a way and a means to communicate with Him.

THE GREAT PLAN

CHAPTER 5
THE MIGHTY DECEIVER
(AKA LUCIFER OR SATAN)

Since the beginning of time, Lucifer and his band of fallen angels have been wreaking havoc throughout the world. Just as the title the *Mighty Deceiver* implies, Satan is the champion of lies. Most are familiar with the name Lucifer or Satan, which he is often referred to as. Interestingly, enough, Lucifer was cast down from heaven as-a-result of his ego.

Once, one of the most majestic angels in the Heavenly realm, Lucifer knew all too well the trappings of the ego. In the beginning, Lucifer was a magnificent being who held a unique ministry in the heavens. He was created by God as all angels were. Originally, he had sat on the right hand of the Father and, as such was most familiar with the mind of Christ. So much so that he began to think that he too, could be Jesus. When Jesus became aware of Lucifer's lofty ambitions, he along with his legion of fallen angels were banished from Heaven and given dominion over the earth.

Man was created in our Father's image and endowed with a human body. A body Satan did not, nor would ever possess. This angered Satan as it elevated man's status above that which was of him. Satan was a Spiritual Being who would never experience the flesh. For this reason, he knew he would need to occupy the mind of man in order to get him to perform his evil works throughout the world. Satan's primary objective was to destroy as many of Jesus' precious souls, having vowed in the end mankind would no longer hold an affinity to Jesus or God for that matter. Yes, he Lucifer, would convince mankind God did not exist which in the end would lead to the destruction of Jesus' beloved souls.

Lucifer, being the father of lies, knew all he had to do to change one's reality was change their perception; *to change how they think.* Perception was high on the list of *extreme weapons,* which he would use to change the hearts and minds of mortal man.

He would use chaos and confusion to ensure division would intensify as wars and rumors of wars would escalate throughout the world. Satan, would use all that was at his disposal on earth such as people, places, and things to infiltrate the minds of the young and old alike.

There would come a time when truth would be hard to come by. More and more people would be hard-pressed to know what the truth was and what it was not. What was once considered right and true will, as a result, become a society filled with self-and-selfish agendas. And so it was, wars and rumors of wars would reach a feverish peak. **Satan knew this final battle could never be won in the flesh. All he needed to do was keep man so distracted with those things of the world he would not understand that he, man, was indeed a Spiritual Being capable of far more than what he believed was humanly possible. He simply needed to provide enough distractions that would preoccupy the minds of men that little time would be spent seeking that which is of the Kingdom of God. So, you see just as Jesus had devised the greatest plan ever known to man, a "*Supreme Plan*", the Mighty Deceiver devised an "*extreme plan*".**

The two greatest deceptions, Lucifer would come to be known for, would be that he and his demons did not truly exist and that man was strictly a physical being incapable of that which is of the spirit. For he knew man was a Spiritual Being capable of far more than what much of mortal man understood.

Additionally, Lucifer would see to it religion would become a thing of the past. He would sow seeds of division among the various religious factions. Most importantly, he did not want man to understand he could have a personal relationship with His Heavenly Father, independent of any specific religion. Lucifer would see to it that religion would assume the role of intercessor between man and the Father. Instead of fostering a relationship with their beloved Father, a relationship would be formed with the church and those whose religious doctrines filled the minds of all who attended. Rather than encouraging a deep and abiding relationship with the Father, a relationship was often formed with those who officiated in the church. Religion had done its very best to minimize the power of the Holy Spirit and how He is alive in the world today.

Jesus knew that soon He would need to remove the veil which had kept His precious souls from understanding what was the true reality. It was not that Jesus had kept secrets from His precious souls, for He knew if the veil had been lifted before the appropriate time the School of Life would no longer be able to serve its purpose, as it was originally intended by the Father.

MY SHADOW MY SOUL

I have a little shadow that goes in and out with me.

I have a little shadow who longs to be set free.

The shadow is my soul who follows me around.

In truth it's here to guide me to

what my soul has found.

The shadow knows the truth and gently tries to guide

me on my way

for he knows that heaven is not where I will stay.

My soul understands my purpose

where often I did not.

Yet that is why I am here to learn that

which must be taught.

That which will enable me to draw ever

closer to the mind of Christ.

To become more enlightened each and every day.

For when I finally learn my lesson,

my soul will find its way.

CHAPTER 6
THE AMBASSADOR OF TRUTH

For everything that is understood by man there is of course an opposite. Therefore, it stands to reason that everything Satan is, Jesus is not. When we want God's honest truths we can go to our Heavenly Father for the answers we are seeking. Answers that would be hard to come by in a world of which man inhabits. There is not a question He will not answer for as Jesus has always said, *"Knock and the door will open, seek and you shall find."*

The truth is, the more you seek the more you will find. Yet, in order to do so man must elevate his thinking. Satan uses all that is of the world; *people, places, and things* **to preoccupy man's mind. In order to activate one's higher conscious, they must be still. Perhaps that is why our Father has said,** *"Be still and KNOW that I am God."* **As it is, in the stillness we can hear what the Father is saying. In these last days, it is imperative one learn to be still rather than do. For it is in the being we will know what**

to do and when to do it as we are led by His magnificent Spirit.

Jesus is available twenty-four hours a day, seven days a week. You do not need a password, a special code, or the latest technical gadget to have a relationship with Him.

Jesus knew there would come a time when mankind would be on the brink of destruction. A time when man's soul will have lost its ability to connect with his Heavenly Father. And so, the primary focus of **Jesus' Great Plan** would be to destroy Lucifer and his legion of fallen angels before Jesus' precious souls became lost throughout eternity.

Jesus had attended to every detail imaginable in His plan to ensure Lucifer and his band of demons would be cast from the earth, at which point, Jesus would establish His Kingdom. Jesus had vowed the earth would never again be destroyed by a flood as in the days of Noah. This time it would be different, for this would be a battle between principalities. This would be a battle that would not be fought in the flesh but in spirit against spirit!

For this reason, Jesus would bring together a Spiritual Army that would be far superior to that which was of mortal man. For this to transpire, many souls would be called to fight in the spirit; to fight a battle of which much would be required.

There would be those, of course, who existed in the spiritual realm, to include St. Michael and many other angelic beings who were highly trained in the *"Art of Spiritual Warfare"*. Additionally, there are those souls, who at the designated time, would inhabit the earth to help prepare the way for Jesus' Kingdom to reign on earth. These souls would be endowed with the very weapons that would be used against Satan and his demons who roamed the earth seeking to destroy God's precious souls.

God's timing would need to be perfect to allow as many souls as possible to take advantage of the School of Life. Very soon, the School of Life would cease to exist, as far too many souls were in danger of losing their way and as a result, unable to find their way back home.

THE GREAT PLAN

CHAPTER 7
THE EGO RULES

As the soul transitions from the spiritual to the human condition he finds himself in, he relies on outside stimuli and, as such is influenced by those things of the world. Gradually, the ego, which provides the foundation for his personality, directs his attention to that which is reflective of man's nature.

The ego seeks self-recognition, as all interests and actions are consumed with self. The ego thrives on competition, often comparing its attributes and successes by the standards of others. As a result, much like Lucifer, he aspires to become equal to if not better than those who viewed him as successful. Because all success at this point is based on outside stimuli, little time is spent on inward speculation. And so, he continues to seek *outside aspirations versus inside inspiration.*

As a result, he confuses happiness with joy looking to people, places, and things to satisfy a longing which comes from deep within his being. Little consideration is given to his true purpose, as there are far too many distractions which have preoccupied the mind keeping him tied to that which is of the material world.

One thing he has discovered, which is constant in life, is that change will most assuredly come at some point. Relationships can change if not altogether be removed through no fault of one's own. For some this can be a life altering event upon which future decisions are made.

As the soul becomes increasingly restless, the human self seeks after material things to find this happiness which seemingly does not last. A vicious cycle then begins as people, places and things change, so does his happiness level.

CHAPTER 8
THE HOLY SPIRIT

We have talked about religion and briefly mentioned the role of the Holy Spirit. *The Holy Spirit is the lifeline for the soul.* When the Holy Spirit is invited to reign, within the center of man's being, He becomes one with His Beloved Father. He then resides within the sanctuary of man, a sanctuary that is often referred to as *the Kingdom within.* The Holy Spirit is the same Spirit who resides in Jesus and the same Spirit who resides in God the Father. How wonderful to know we too can have access to the Spirit of our Heavenly Father.

The Holy Spirit is a gift from our Heavenly Father. The soul has always understood he, is in fact, a Spiritual Being who is one in the Spirit with our Heavenly Father. Because the soul does not remember previous lifetimes, nor that he is a Citizen of Heaven, it is crucial the soul be able to communicate with the Divine. *The Holy Spirit is a help mate, a teacher, a friend, a comforter, in whom the soul can confide. One can say the Holy Spirit*

is the constant gardener of one's soul. For this connection to be made, man must become less enthralled with that of the exterior. As time has progressed on earth it has become increasingly difficult for the soul to connect with His Beloved Father. There are far too many distractions in today's world that keeps one from being able to hear what the Spirit is saying. In years past, it was easier for man to respond to the still voice within, encouraging man to explore a deeper and more meaningful way of life. Jesus knew how very important the Holy Spirit was to one's soul, as did He not say to the disciples prior to His final ascension that, ***"It indeed is far better that I leave so another can take My place."*** Jesus knew the comfort the Holy Spirit would be to all who believed in Him.

In the normal course of a lifetime, while enrolled in the School of Life, man has become less and less content with those things of the world. As a result, he begins to experience an increasing restlessness. There is a longing that comes from deep within that cannot seemingly be satisfied, and so it is he is no longer content with the world he has built for himself.

He intrinsically feels there must be something more and begins to question his purpose for being. Although he does not yet understand he is being influenced by the promptings from his soul, he begins to understand there is so much more to his mortal life than what he had previously understood.

Many times, this understanding is influenced by an event or personal experience which has greatly impacted the foundation upon which he has built his life. It often takes an **"ah-ha"** moment to awaken what has laid dormant within. Man begins to seek after that which he had not paid attention to in the past, and so the second part of his earthly journey begins.

This is the part of the journey where man realizes he is indeed at a crossroads. He begins to ask the question, **"Who am I really?"** He is no longer satisfied with the person he has allowed others to see. A person who has been shaped primarily by the reactions and opinions of others. Yes, a person who has centered his life upon the standards set by mankind. Standards that often went against what he knew to be morally right and true.

There is now an increased desire to separate himself from those things which do not fulfill the deepest desires of his heart to materialize. He is no longer willing to conform to someone else's dreams or desires. It is at this point he turns inward for the answers and guidance he is seeking. This is when, with the help of the Holy Spirit, he discovers what he is most enthusiastic about!

Enthusiasm is always present when one discovers that which his soul is longing to complete; that which is his sole purpose for being. The soul will now be able to assume its rightful position within his being, no longer content to take a backseat in which he has found himself. This is when he begins to celebrate his own uniqueness as he gives freely of the gifts and talents which have been given freely unto him. He is no longer willing to march to the beat of a different drummer.

This self-discovery is prompted by the Holy Spirit in those who have accepted Jesus Christ as their Savior. Having opened the lines of communication to the Father, he now starts to see himself and the world through a different set of eyes. It is the same with hearing as he must now exercise his spiritual ears to hear what is coming from the sanctuary within.

The more time we spend in communion with the Holy Spirit the better we will understand those characteristics which exemplify the Divine. It is through this communion we develop a desire to become more like our Heavenly Father. It is through the Holy Spirit we become molded and shaped into our Father's image. This is when we begin to understand and accept our Father's will. As our understanding increases, the *Fruits of the Spirit* become more prevalent within one's being.

This is a newfound freedom man has not experienced before. One that will enable him to eventually transition from that which is of the physical to his true nature of a Spiritual Being. *To do so he must combine his talents with his Spiritual Gifts as he moves forward to his true purpose for being. That which is his destiny!*

INVITATION FROM THE HOLY SPIRIT

Won't you come and sit with me
and lay your head to rest?
For surely you must see I know,
that you have tried your best.
The door is always open so
won't you please come in?
I know you better than you know yourself
and where your soul has been.
Yet, I am near you always as you
journey in this life,
A journey which at times may seem
is always filled with strife.
That is why I am here for you
as you travel down this path,
As this is where you will find a joy that will surely last.
And when you're feeling rested
and it is time for you to go remember,
There is something I want your soul to know.
I will never leave you of this you need not fear,
For no matter where life takes you, I am always here.

PART 2

THE GREAT PLAN

CHAPTER 9
THE TRUTH WILL SET YOU FREE

Now that you have been given a brief overview of not only who and what you truly are, we will now elaborate on our Father's Great Plan. This plan is the plan that when fully implemented will lead to the destruction of Lucifer and his legion of fallen angels.

As you now know the School of Life has existed on earth for well over 2000 years. This school was developed by our Heavenly Father to help further each soul's education as well as provide each soul with an opportunity to become more fully enlightened in the ways of our Heavenly Father. It is important to note that no soul was ever forced to attend, yet all souls considered it a great opportunity to perfect that which attending the School of Life would offer.

Because Satan ruled the earth, he was of course the very embodiment of everything Jesus was not. To say that Satan was immensely jealous of mankind, is in truth, an understatement for Satan knew man's status was well above that which was of his spirit. Having sat at the right hand of the Father, he understood the mind of Jesus, and now he knew how to captivate the mind of man by using his conscious mind to keep him from being connected to the mind of Christ. In doing so, he would hold man hostage to that which was of the world; to that which the ego would find not only enticing but immensely satisfying. For everything the ego is the soul is not.

Religion had played a major role in mankind not fully embracing or understanding what is the reality. Since many did not understand they were in fact a Spiritual Being, man identified with self and all that was of the ego. The ego of course being something Satan was more than familiar with.

Far too many religions were unaware of the School of Life as it was originally created by God. A school of which, should a soul desire, could be attended multiple times throughout eternity. Although there were some religions in the Eastern part of the world who understood the true meaning and purpose of reincarnation, there were just as many who did not. More found this to be a most preposterous idea. Some would go so far as to exclaim that since reincarnation was not mentioned in the Bible, it did not exist.

However, it was interesting that up until the middle of the second century reincarnation was included in the Christian doctrines. These teachings were banned in order to stop people from conducting a serious spiritual inquiry about their Divine origins and the ultimate purpose of life on earth.

I will tell you that all souls possess an inner knowing, which is not to be confused with specific memories of past lifetimes while attending the School of Life. Yet, there are many who have experienced what is referred to as a *"Déjà Vu"* moment. This is the feeling you have already experienced something even though your conscious mind says you have not. This then is where **_Sensititus Divinitius_** comes into play. *This is the Divine Instinct all humans are endowed with.* This, of course, is not a sense which the physical body depends on for survival, and as such is used infrequently if not at all. Interestingly, this Divine Instinct, at one point was acknowledged as a spiritual connection, yet just as reincarnation was no longer to be acknowledged the same was to be said for the Divine Instinct within each and every being.

So, you can begin to understand how religion has, in fact, altered that which is the reality. That which once was a very important key to one's spiritual development.

When Jesus began formulating his Great Plan, He knew there would be a time when the veil would need to be lifted. There would come a time when evil will have reached such a feverish point man would be hard pressed to discover what was of His true nature. A time when man would no longer be able to determine *right from wrong nor wrong from right.* He knew there would be many souls who would elect to be on earth for what some would refer to as, "The Awakening". This would require there would be those souls who resided on earth to understand the essence of not only who they truly were but the precise role they would play in the battle between good and evil. There were, as a result, various positions that would need to be filled by those who understood the meaning of the times and what they would be facing.

One such position that would need to be filled was that which would come to be referred to as "Earth Angels". This position had never existed before. There were many reasons for this as it created a great deal of consternation among the Senior Angels in Heaven.

One must understand angels were created for the distinct purpose of serving their Heavenly Father. They were Spiritual Beings who were highly enlightened in the ways of their Creator desiring only to serve Him. They were not endowed with free will such as man experienced as the only will angelic beings sought was that of Jesus, Himself.

And so, when Jesus said He was going to send an angel to earth to take up temporary residence in a human body the Senior Angels could not understand the benefit of doing so. They knew that an important part of the human condition required one would be endowed with free will. This will, of course, was far different than the will of the Heavenly Father. Since the human condition required the soul would not remember from where it had come, it seemed like it would be a strong disadvantage for an *Earth Angel.* An angel that had never desired anything but that which was in the will of their Heavenly Father.

Many in the Heavens felt to do so was not only impossible but cruel. Why should an angel be subjected to situations they had never experienced before? Would they not be subjected to more than what an angelic being should be required to endure?

Jesus patiently listened to their concerns, yet He would not be swayed from that which He felt would be necessary to help prepare the way for His Kingdom to reign on earth.

He explained He would make certain every *Earth Angel* would have what they needed when they needed it. This was something He would personally attend to. Additionally, He would assign a guardian angel to watch over each and every *Earth Angel* in their earthly duties. Duties He would ensure they were well trained for prior to their arrival on earth.

CHAPTER 10
THE SELECTION

Jesus would now post His newly formed position of an *Earth Angel*. All applicants would be considered and encouraged to inquire within. In simple language, the posting stated ***"Looking for angels who are willing to help prepare the way for My Kingdom to reign on earth. This is a newly created position, which will require much of an angelic being. They will play a most important role in preparing the way for My Kingdom to reign on earth."***

When Wendy saw the posting she was most intrigued. Never having experienced life as a human being, it seemed like an opportunity of a lifetime for her. The very thought of helping Jesus prepare the way for His Kingdom on earth was something all in the spiritual world had anxiously been looking forward to. Never did it occur to her that she, Wendy, would be able to participate in.

When Wendy was called in for the interview with Jesus her enthusiasm was such that she could hardly contain herself. She was so excited over the prospect of being sent to earth as a human she overlooked a most important detail. A detail which would create a great deal of anguish in her role as a human being.

As an angel Wendy did not fully understand the important role free will played in the development of one's lesson plan in the School of Life. Never having experienced life as a human being, she could only relate to her desire to fulfill the will of her Heavenly Father. She could not possibly see that free will would be a very difficult lesson and one she herself would come to understand as part of the human condition. This understanding would be a very hard lesson for an angel, let alone a human being.

It was with much naivety, and of course, the desire to please the Father, Wendy enthusiastically accepted this most esteemed position. Perhaps, though, esteemed is not the correct word. Webster defines esteemed as: *held in great respect, admired.*

Now, in retrospect, if Wendy were to review what she once thought one would consider to be esteemed, she would indeed see that Jillian, her angelic sister, responded to Wendy's enthusiastic position as though she did indeed have, as the saying goes *"rocks in her head"*.

Jillian and Wendy had been together since the beginning of time. What one lacked the other made up for, and so it was that many in the heavens admired the work they accomplished together in various capacities. Capacities which, of course, always reflected the will of the beloved Father. When Wendy applied for the position of Earth Angel, Jillian was most reluctant to follow suit.

Perhaps better than Wendy, Jillian understood the ramifications of what it meant to be fully human. And from what she could see there were many obstacles which any angel would be hard pressed to overcome. Especially when she heard an *Earth Angel* would not initially remember where they had come from and would no longer embrace the will of their Heavenly Father.

Never had Jillian dug her heels in as she had at that moment. Wendy on the other hand never considered Jillian would not be by her side. Jesus, you must understand, already anticipated Jillian's response knowing her reluctance would work out to His

46

advantage. And so for the first time ever, Wendy and Jillian went their separate ways. But not for long!

Jesus knew Jillian would eventually succumb, as she knew together they were a mighty fortress that no man could stop. It would not be until many years later, upon earth, they would reconnect, once again, to become a force mortal man could not reckon with nor stop.

Every soul received intense training for the mission they would be required to accomplish on earth. This training for each *Earth Angel* could be different depending on what they were sent to accomplish. Wendy and Jillian were to receive in-depth training in a subject which much of mankind confused with happiness. That subject was "JOY". While joy for an angel was a feeling they were most familiar with, it of course, was not the same for mankind. Because angels lived to serve their Heavenly Father, they experienced a level of joy that one does not experience on earth. This is because together they are one with the Spirit of their beloved Jesus. Joy was a natural result of sharing in all that was of their Heavenly Father, never seeking nor questioning that which was not within His perfect will.

Wendy and Jillian must understand the joy they naturally experienced, as an angel, was elusive for a vast majority of humans, and as such would be well trained in *"The Art of Joy-filled Living"*, which they would soon discover was not easily accomplished on earth.

There were a multitude of reasons for this, as human beings often confused happiness with joy. Happiness was, of course, based on people, places and things. All that was of the exterior. Satan who held dominion over the earth would use all that was of the world to see to it man approached life from the outside in, rather than, seek that which was of the Father's Kingdom which of course is where joy could be found.

Both Wendy and Jillian understood the urgency of the times in which they would be asked to serve. They knew the battle on earth was intensifying. Quite simply put, these would be desperate times that would require desperate measures. Measures that would require much innovation. Innovation that resulted in *Earth*

Angels, who over time, would be scattered throughout the world.

Never having experienced life as a human, there would be a period of time in which each would need to fully experience the human condition. Since they would not remember from where they had come, they would, of course, depend on free will for the choices they too would make while in the human condition. For without this experience they would not be able to understand the difficult lessons man would face as-a-result of their choices. This would be the same for *Earth Angels* as well. They would learn what was necessary in order to accomplish their assigned task as an *Earth Angel.*

One could say experience is the best teacher, and so it was the case for both Wendy and Jillian. It would be many years before Wendy and Jillian would reunite on earth, which would result in the formation of ABBA and Company. A company in which they would teach about one subject and one subject only. The subject of course being "joy". In essence, they would teach all about *joy and the Holy Spirit.* **And as we have said before, the Holy Spirit was indeed a subject**

that mankind, in the end, would need to become most familiar with if he was to survive what was to come!

When Wendy and Jillian reunited each intrinsically felt there was a deep connection between the two of them. A connection they did not fully understand in the beginning, but none the less, experienced. It is important to see how the Holy Spirit moves in the world today. For Jillian and Wendy to reconnect on earth was nothing short of **Divine Providence**. It would take a deliberate act of God for this reunion to occur. It would take well over thirty mortal years for this reunion to take place, although neither, fully realized, they had in fact, been together in their Father's Kingdom. This knowledge would be revealed later by none other than Jesus Himself.

THE GREAT PLAN

CHAPTER 11

THE REUNION

Without wanting to waste time going into too much detail regarding their earthly reunion, it is important to note that Wendy and Jillian lived at opposite ends of the state. Both worked for the same corporation, and it was through their earthly jobs Jesus would reacquaint the two.

Wendy was becoming increasingly restless in her job, longing to strike out on her own to use her own gifts and talents for the betterment of mankind. And so it was, she gave notice on her job which required her position be filled. It was Jillian, who resided at the opposite end of the state, who applied. One, of course, would wonder that if Wendy were to leave the company, how on earth could they form an alliance? It was once again the Holy Spirit who intervened. Wendy was required to do an exit interview with Senior Management. Never in her wildest imagination would Wendy have thought she would change her mind. Yet, change her mind she did, resulting in her accepting another position within the corporation. As a result,

Wendy and Jillian became fast friends. It wasn't long before they realized they were kindred spirits. Both had a strong desire to encourage others to use their gifts and talents for the betterment of mankind. This was how ABBA and Company came to pass. A company in which they would teach about *"The Art of Joy-filled Living"*. Little did they understand what an undertaking this would be.

There will be those "Doubting Thomas's" who would have a difficult time believing what came next for Wendy and Jillian. This book is not for those who are unwilling to explore that which is not only possible but also the reality.

It is important to clarify *Earth Angels are Spiritual Beings who have been sent to earth to share God's messages with the world*. Such was the case for Wendy and Jillian. Jesus had assured the Senior Angels in Heaven, Wendy and Jillian, would have what they needed when they would need it.

For this reason, it was important both understood the importance of the relationship they had formed. It was this initial visit from Jesus that would lead Wendy and Jillian to understand their mission on earth had indeed begun in the heavens above.

Wendy and Jillian were shopping in the local grocery store when a man approached them and asked if they were sisters, as they resembled one another so very much. Without looking up Wendy replied, **"Yes they were."** They had been asked this by others, so many times before so it was simply easier to reply yes. It was then Wendy looked up and standing before them was none other than, you guessed it, Jesus Himself. **"Oh, no!"**, thought Wendy, **"I just lied to our Blessed Savior."** He then replied. *"Well, if you two are not sisters you must have been together for a very long time as you resemble each other so."*

It was when Jesus gazed into each of their eyes it was as if He looked right through their eyes. It was a look which penetrated deep within the recesses of their souls. Jesus then asked, *"If there was a local Chinese store close by?" as He understood the oil was indeed cheaper there.* And with that He was gone.

Jillian tried to follow Him but just as quickly as He had appeared, Jesus disappeared. It would not be until many years later they would truly understand the full meaning of the words Jesus spoke.

If Jesus had not appeared in front of the two of them it would have been easy for one to think what had happened was just a figment of their imagination. Both together had witnessed what many would say was not humanly possible.

Jesus had not yet lifted the veil which had kept mankind from understanding what truly was the reality. Jesus knew there would be circumstances that would need to take place before the veil could finally be removed. However, in the case of Wendy and Jillian, it was important they begin to understand the reality of not only who they were but what would be required of each of them.

CHAPTER 12
THE PURPOSE BEHIND JOY

When ABBA and Company was formed it would serve in two capacities. One which ABBA in the secular world would stand for "A Better Business Alternative" and the other in the non-secular world was ABBA which of course means "Father". For this reason, they needed to develop a mission statement that would explain the purpose for ABBA and Company. The Mission Statement would read as follows:

ABBA and Company Mission Statement ABBA and Company has been formed as a result of its SUPREME commitment to the betterment of mankind. The primary objective is to teach others to maximize their potential for the good of self and others. ABBA and Company believe all individuals are created with an inherent gift which when nurtured and encouraged will provide a significant contribution towards the improvement of mankind.

Having experienced working in the secular world both Wendy and Jillian could see how the ego often overlooked the natural gifts and talents of man. The ego often would create barriers to that which would fulfill the intense desires the soul was longing to complete. Wendy and Jillian understood that no matter what one's job was the soul understood his purpose as a Spiritual Being. It would be their role to help all understand that every being is endowed with their own unique gifts and talents, and when encouraged to do so would contribute greatly to the world in which they found themselves in. They understood the basic nature of mankind is intrinsically good. Of course, the key word here is *intrinsic*.

Never could Wendy nor Jillian have ever realized, prior to forming ABBA, how much of mankind confused "joy" with happiness. For many the subject of Joy was associated with religion. A subject that was not to be approached in one's everyday work environment. It was as a result difficult for an employer to see how the "*Art of Joy-filled Living*" could benefit the goals which a company was trying to achieve. Although Wendy and Jillian managed to present a few select seminars such as "*Joy in the Workplace*" it did not prosper as one would have thought. This was especially difficult for Wendy and Jillian to understand as they knew the magnitude of joy and what an important role it would play in the ensuing years.

Wendy and Jillian then turned their attention to the non-secular arena. Once again this proved to be quite challenging as far too many religions were unwilling to listen to anything outside of their specific doctrine. As hard as they would try, they could see how much the ego had infiltrated the church. Those in positions of authority were unwilling to invite speakers or programs which they were not familiar with.

This was a time when man was very much enthralled with all that money could buy. Success was based on status, material wealth and all that would benefit self and selfish interests. Having formed ABBA and Company in 1990, religion had already begun to become less important as man became consumed with worldly matters rather than with that of a spiritual or Godly nature.

Happiness was based on worldly pursuits and pleasures which left less and less time for inward introspection. Satan had done his best to discourage a relationship with the Heavenly Father. All Satan needed to do was hold man hostage by the things of the world. Consumerism was at an all-time high, and so it was when one lost interest in a particular thing or person, he would simply seek after that which would provide him with the happiness he was so desperately seeking. Of course, as Jillian and Wendy knew the happiness humans sought after was elusive, as when circumstances changed one's happiness level changed as well.

Even though there were many times in which they were discouraged, neither of them had ever considered giving up. As you will soon discover, as you continue to read the following pages, **that which is Divinely inspired by God, will endure.**

Over the upcoming years Wendy and Jillian were to encounter various circumstances that would guide them in their mission as they held on fast to, what they often referred to, in the upcoming years, as the wings of a dove (*a dove of course, being synonymous with the Holy Spirit*).

In the beginning there was another very important encounter, once again, with a messenger from God. This second encounter would again prove to be most important as it was indeed the message that would refer to "**The Great Plan**".

On this particular day, Wendy and Jillian were eating at a local restaurant discussing, once again, how they would be able to accomplish what the Lord had sanctioned them for. It was at this time a Merchant Seaman, or so He said He was, sat down at the counter next to Wendy. On the other side, a man who was of an evil persuasion sat next to Jillian.

The Merchant Seaman asked Wendy if she was a writer of which she quickly replied, *"No I am not."* At this point both He and Jillian chimed in saying, ***"Yes, yes, you are."*** He then proceeded to share the story of how He had been up for a promotion as Captain of the ship and had hurt His back, and as a result was now working part time so He could write in the evenings. This sounded most familiar to Wendy as she was now working part time at her previous company in order to sustain an income. As such, she was not able to give her full attention to ABBA and Company. He then kept insisting Wendy was indeed a writer and that she and Jillian would remember every bit of the following conversation well into the future.

He spoke of **Dorothy Day** who had been writing what He referred to as *"The Great Plan"*. He concluded by saying that there would come a time when the three of them would be together in a taxi cab and Jesus would be in the driver's seat and Wendy and Jillian would be in the back. The cab would become surrounded, but they were not to get out of the car.

With that He stood up and walked away, much the same as the first encounter. He simply disappeared. Interestingly, at the same time He disappeared the man of evil persuasion disappeared as well.

Wendy and Jillian did not understand why He was referring to *Dorothy Day* nor the book *"The Great Plan"*. They searched many bookstores trying to locate such a book that had been written. Interestingly enough, there was no such book that existed! In researching *Dorothy Day's* life, she was known as a Social Activist and co-founder of the *Catholic Worker Movement*, promoting pacifism, Catholic social teachings, and direct aid to the poor, and she also worked through newspapers and houses of hospitality for the poor and homeless. She dedicated her life fighting for Social Justice for the poor advocating for peace, non-violence and human rights. She was a strong advocate for pacifism, opposing all forms of war and violence including "nuclear weapons".

It is clear to conclude that for pacifism to manifest, no battle could be overcome unless the sinful dispositions of men could be subdued by love. Evil could only be exterminated from the earth by goodness. It is foolish to rely upon the flesh to preserve man from harm. There is great security in being gentle, harmless, long suffering and abundant in mercy. Therefore, *it is only the meek who shall inherit the earth.* For the violent will resort to the sword and perish with the sword. As you can assuredly see, *Dorothy Day* understood no earthly battle would ever be won in the flesh for in the end it would be the *Fruits of the Spirit* that will insure victory. As we will soon see, these gifts will play a major role in the Heavenly Father's *Great Plan!* For these are the mighty weapons found within the Kingdom of God.

A Kingdom which reigns within all who accept Jesus Christ as their Heavenly Savior! **"Yes"**, thought Wendy, **"the pieces of the puzzle are now starting to come together."** It never dawned on

Wendy that she and Jillian would be responsible for writing **"The *Great Plan"*** as narrated by non-other than the Holy Spirit.

It is important to remember God's timing in *Jesus' Great Plan*. Before it can be revealed to mankind, there must be circumstances that are allowed to transpire for one to understand what is the reality. For Jesus knew once this was revealed *all hell would break lose on earth.*

CHAPTER 13
ROME WASN'T BUILT IN A DAY

In the beginning, God created heaven and the earth and then along came man. Man was and has always been created in our Father's image. Yet, no matter how beautifully and wonderfully man was made, evil would become ever present throughout our Father's creation. It would become increasingly difficult for one's soul to be able to acquire those *Fruits of the Spirit* which are of the Heavenly Father. As far back as one can remember religion achieved the exact opposite of what our Heavenly Father intended. Religion was used as a means to control man's ability to form a lasting and abiding relationship with his beloved Father. The Bible provides many examples of man's fight against those who ruled by the ego, and yes, that which is of self and selfish agendas. As a result, wars and rumors of wars have existed since the beginning of time. To say that man is born into sin is, indeed, valid as mankind is born into a sinful world.

Jesus knew He would be able to use the world to teach man's precious souls those ideals/ fruits which exemplified the mind of Christ. Our Lord, being the Supreme Being of all mankind, would use what was created to His utmost advantage. And so it was, when Satan was banished to earth, He would use the ego, which Satan was most familiar with, to His Supreme advantage. Jesus knew the nature of the beast is what man would need to understand in order to seek that which was of his true nature; that of a Spiritual Being.

Our Father knew for everything there is indeed an exact opposite. You cannot know one or fully understand one until you know the other. Jesus would use man's ego, which was of Satan's world, to provide the perfect opportunity for man's soul to advance in his spiritual education. It was the School of Life that was the perfect place for a soul to become more fully enlightened as a Spiritual Being.

Over time, Jesus knew Satan would take full advantage of that which he could avail himself of while on earth. Satan had devised a plan, which if successful, would ensure Jesus' precious souls would be forever lost in the ways of our Heavenly Father. His main goal was to convince man God did not exist, and as a result, God's precious souls would be destroyed.

The same as Satan had an **extreme plan** of which every detail would be attended to, Jesus had a **Supreme Plan** that would take full advantage of the weapons Satan would use against His beloved souls.

Jesus watched as the various details of Satan's plan began to unfold. As in any battle, timing is the key. Jesus would, therefore, keep the School of Life operating until it could no longer accomplish that which it was originally intended for. Satan, as a result, would become prideful and filled with lofty ambitions that had previously produced the desired results he anticipated. What he did not and could not know is his ego, once again, would prove to be the downfall of a plan of which he was certain could not and would not fail.

It is imperative one be most familiar with the *Fruits of the Spirit* for they are the weapons that in the end will stand strong against the evil one and his legion of fallen angels. Satan would use man's ego to carry out those actions which are nonexistent in our Father's Kingdom. All in all, the reality is the *Fruits of the Spirit* will be the traits responsible for preparing the way for our Father's Kingdom to reign on earth as it is in heaven.

CHAPTER 14
THE DEVIL MADE ME DO IT!

Throughout history Satan/Lucifer has often been referred to as the devil. Webster defines devil as: *something that is morally wrong, wicked or harmful.* He encompasses actions, characters or situations that cause pain and suffering or in-justice. For a moment let us look at what Webster has to say about Satan. Webster defines Satan as*: a powerful, evil spirit and the adversary of God. Satan is therefore, the tempter of humanity.* Now, let us examine the definition of evil. Webster defines evil as*: profound immorality especially when regarded as a supernatural force.* Because evil is often defined as a supernatural force, it is difficult for man to wrap his arms around such a description.

Let us then see what the Bible defines supernatural as: *phenomena or entities that are beyond or outside the laws of nature and human understanding.* Supernatural is what he is naturally endowed with. The devil understood once man embraced his true identity, of a Spiritual Being, he would no longer fight the enemy in the flesh as it would prove to be, in the end, an exercise in futility. This would be a battle that would necessitate what man would refer to as supernatural, yet perfectly natural for a Spiritual Being.

In order to know how, as a Spiritual Being, to fight against evil, one must understand the weapons Satan and his legion would use against Jesus' precious souls. The weapons of a Spiritual Being are those strengths and ideals of our Heavenly Father. These are weapons of which mortal man generally does not consider in a battle.

When you think of the weapons the devil will use, interestingly enough, a great deal of the weapons used start with the letter "**D**". Let us examine a few such weapons:

Distractions: play a major role in Satan's arsenal as he has full access to all that is of the world using people, places, and things to occupy the minds of man.

Division: is now seen throughout the world. Religion, government and relationships are becoming unduly effected decreasing one's ability to resist that which is not in mankind's highest interest.

Depression: is being manipulated through substances and social networks creating barriers to that which is of our Father's Spirit. "Joy" is severely impaired as the soul is unable to connect with the Spirit of our living God.

Despair: to give up on, hopelessness.

Discouragement: a loss of confidence, enthusiasm.

Downtrodden: suppressed, treated badly by people.

Demolish: completely destroy.

There are many more weapons which the enemy is proficient in. We have been shown for everything Satan is, Jesus is not. So let us examine the weapons we as a Spiritual Being can use against the weapons of the adversary. As I have mentioned there are many **Fruits of the Spirit** which are in Jesus' spiritual arsenal.

Distractions: **Self-control,** when exercised, will enable one to resist temptation and worldly influences that can lead to a distracted and unfocused life.

Division: **Peace** is a powerful antidote to conflict and division.

Depression: **Joy** is an effective antidote as it comes from a relationship with our Heavenly Father and can be found in the Kingdom within.

Despair: **Faith** that all things work together for good.

Discouragement: **Patience** and **long suffering** which allows us to maintain a positive outlook to endure trials and suffering.

Downtrodden: *Long suffering*. The ability to deal with difficult people

Demolish: **The Fruits of the Spirit!**

THE DEVIL MADE ME DO IT

The devil made me do it said the spider to the fly. The devil made me do it as he went buzzing by.

So, I'll just sit and wait awhile as you climb up that big oak tree and then I'll spin a web so tight you never will get free.

The fly was on the lookout for all that was around. I'll be safe for sure he thought if I don't fly near the ground.

I'll just climb this big oak tree and lay my head a bit to rest, surely no harm will come to me as I settle near this nest.

He didn't see what was coming as the spider circled round and so it would have been far better had he stayed closer to the ground.

Better safe than sorry said the spider to the fly, for you see I was watching as you went buzzing by.

Best to be on the lookout for those who are around, truly would have been best for you if you had stayed closer to the ground. -Wendy

As you can see for every weapon the enemy throws at us, we have an arsenal of weapons which are of the Holy Spirit. These weapons will counteract any weapon the devil will use against Jesus' people. Those who have chosen to be on earth in these last days are aware of the weapons which are of the Holy Spirit. Weapons which are a result of what each has perfected while enrolled in the School of Life. These weapons are not to be confused with your Spiritual Gifts, but rather, ones you have learned and now are being called to put into action as you help prepare the way for our Father's Kingdom to reign on earth!

It is imperative we understand the enemy is here in our midst constantly trying to **distract**, **deter** and yes, **destroy**. One must be mindful paying close attention to all that surrounds them.

As a Spiritual Being one understands two wrongs will never make a right. Two wrongs can lead to a world that starves the soul of the essence of his being. What once was revered as right and true, is now cut off from the Divine. As this multiplies, what was created in our Father's image no longer resembles that of His original creation.

The ***Fruits of the Spirit*** that many a soul have worked diligently to acquire in the School of Life, are at an extreme disadvantage if unable to connect with the Holy Spirit. This, of course, is the primary objective in Satan's ***"extreme plan"***. Experience is indeed the best teacher, yet when one is not allowed or able to share this knowledge it becomes a no-win situation. Because these fruits exemplify the ideals of our Heavenly Father, Satan will do all in his power to subdue if not destroy these ideals which are prevalent in our Father's Kingdom.

THE GREAT PLAN

CHAPTER 15

THE SPIRITUAL WARRIOR, COULD THIS BE YOU?

It is crucial one must understand the important role a **Spiritual Warrior** plays in the battle between good and evil. There are a multitude of angels who had been actively engaged in a battle of which much of mankind had not participated in. There is an ongoing spiritual battle between angels and demons with angels fighting against evil forces in the heavenly realm. Yes, a battle that is between principalities and will never be won in the flesh. Satan and his legion have always understood the mechanics of working, not only in the material plain, but in the spiritual plain as well. This meant he and his demonic forces could move in and out of these dimensions as well as use people, places and things to do his dirty works. There is such evil of which mankind would be hard pressed to imagine much less know who and what to fight against. You, as a Spiritual Warrior, must now play an active role in our *Father's Supreme Army.*

Never doubt you have been well trained for combat. Your armor is the shield of Christ, which will protect you as the battle intensifies in the days and the weeks to come. Those of you who are called to actively participate in this battle know who you are. As a Spiritual Warrior you are well-versed in the powers you possess as a Spiritual Being and are now being called to *active duty.* Webster defines active duty as: *an activity at a particular place or a particular way to engage in physical pursuits, as well as spiritual.* As a Spiritual Warrior you are part of a *special task force.* You are specifically trained for this mission. Your time on earth has provided in-depth training that has been necessary in order for you to understand the weapons Satan and his legion will use against My warriors. Perhaps another way to look at your life experience would be more appropriately labeled as *"Boot Camp"* (a rigorous course of training). Your time on earth has provided you with the necessary training to increase or significantly affect your knowledge and abilities. It has been said, *"Experience is the best teacher."* These experiences enable you to become wise in the ways of the enemy as a Spiritual Warrior.

You understand knowledge and wisdom are two entirely different things. You are endowed with an inner knowing. This inner knowing comes from within and cannot be acquired from the exterior. This knowing is the result of your spirit being one with our Father. As the Commander-In-Chief of the *Supreme Army,* it is imperative a *Spiritual Warrior* be able to adhere to those ideals which are of the mind of Christ. Jesus resides in the very center of every warrior proclaiming, "**I am in you, and you are in Me, therefore, all that I am, you are, all that I have you have.**"

You have all you need to be an effective warrior. As a *Spiritual Warrior* you must trust you will have what you need when you need it. You are well armed with the gifts and talents for which you have been called. You are now being called to *active duty. Spiritual Warriors* are equipped with the ears to hear what our Father, the Commander-In-Chief, is saying, and the eyes to see what needs to be seen. Jesus is the Commander-In-Chief of His Supreme Army. He is, of course, The Ambassador of Truth. The purpose of life is to *learn, to serve, and to grow.* Now is the time you must put what you have learned into practice. It is time to serve in the greatest army of all time. Jesus, as your Commander-In-Chief, will lead you into victory. This is a victory well worth fighting for. In the end, Jesus' Kingdom will reign on earth as it is in Heaven.

As a Spiritual Warrior you have the eyes to see that which mortal man cannot. Jesus said, ***"Because I am in you, and you are in Me you will automatically respond as My Spirit guides you."*** It is crucial that you disengage from those emotions that will create barriers to your ability to defend against the weapons Satan and his legion will use against you. Chaos and confusion are not of the Divine. Jesus is the Ambassador of Truth and the Commander-In-Chief of this Supreme Army. You must utilize the weapons that you are well versed in. The enemy's primary objective is to destroy as many souls as possible before Jesus' return to earth. As a Spiritual Warrior you must maintain an offensive posture at all times. You must use your spiritual eyes to see that which others cannot. In doing so, you will be able to stand strong against the weapons he will use against His chosen. Jesus will use Satan's attacks to His

Supreme advantage. Because His warriors are well-aware they are Spiritual Beings, they are now able to fight effectively. Jesus will use Satan's attacks to awaken the souls of His people.

Jesus' *Spiritual Warriors* are able to move in and out of the spiritual plain. Those who have been called to *active duty* are able to fight on two fronts. One being the physical realm and the other being the spiritual realm. Having this two-fold ability is causing Satan to intensify his attacks. Satan and his legion are now devouring the souls who are not protected by our Father's Holy breastplate. Because these souls have lost their connection to the Father, they are easily distracted by thoughts which are of darkness. The number of disconnected souls is increasing as the time of Jesus' return draws near. As *Spiritual Warriors*, you must surround yourself with those of like minds and purpose. *Spiritual Warriors* must rely strongly on one another in order to present a formidable force against the enemy.

As your Commander-In-Chief, Jesus has formed the greatest Supreme Army of all time. You are being summoned to *active duty*. Each of you has been specifically trained in your *spiritual gifts.* When you use these gifts, in combination with others, it will result in an army far superior to that which is of mortal man. As a result, you will not perform as a separate or singular entity, but rather as a superior force that mankind has not experienced nor conceived of before! Every strategic move has been well planned by our Commander-In-Chief. You must now use your gifts according to our Father's plan!

As Jesus has said, ***"He that is in Me is far greater than he that is of the world."*** Every detail is being attended to. To be effective, it is imperative you respond to that which your soul is ready to confront. Many times, man has exclaimed there is strength in numbers. Those who are of His Supreme Army are not ruled by that which is of the ego. And so it is, there is a bond, a union, which Satan and his legion cannot defeat. For the weapons they use cannot penetrate that which Jesus' mighty army is prepared for.

The battle you, as a *Spiritual Warrior,* are engaged in is not like any physical battle known to man. Now you, as a *Spiritual Warrior,* will be using weapons which are far superior to that which can be found on earth. Although your body resides on earth, you will have access to those weapons much of mortal man does not. Jesus has formed a covenant with each of His Warriors promising *you would have all you need at your disposal.*

There will be certain events to come which man would consider to be supernatural. You who know who you are, as a *Spiritual Being,* will see that which man labels as supernatural will, indeed, be natural for you! You will join forces with *Spiritual Beings* who are no longer walking this earth. Saint Michael, along with his legion of war angels, will fight side-by-side with Jesus' *Spiritual Warriors* inhabiting the earth. Together, this mighty army will slay the demons whom man cannot see.

Satan, the Mighty Deceiver, will no longer keep Jesus' chosen from all they have access to as a Spiritual Being. His timing is precise, and so it is time to use the full force of His *Supreme Army* against the Prince of Darkness.

<u>Characteristics of a Spiritual Warrior</u>

A True Spiritual Warrior:

1. *knows himself well. In doing so he can assess his strengths and weaknesses.*
2. *knows the enemy will use, whenever possible, his own gifts against him in an effort to   keep him from using his gifts as our Father intended.*
3. *is not afraid to stand up for what is right knowing when he does, he will stand out for all to see.*
4. *is at the Father's disposal 24 hours a day.*
5. *is relentless in his pursuit of the enemy.*
6. *is not afraid to lead by example.*
7. *embraces our Father's will above all else.*
8. *is not driven by that which is of the ego.*
9. *is not afraid to look at that which others close their eyes too.*
10. *understands all our responsible for how they respond.*
11. *understands this is a battle between principalities.*
12. *will keep on fighting no matter what the cost until he is certain Satan and his legion are destroyed once and for all.*

13. *is willing to take the place on a battlefield of a wounded brother or sister.*

As Spiritual Warriors we need to understand this battle is not about flesh and blood but against the powers in heavenly places. The enemy is able to move against us in the physical realm. There are forces we cannot see that are actively working around us. The enemy will attack God's Army by using people, places, and things to steal the hearts of Jesus' people away from Him.

These types of battles are fought in the physical world but involve spiritual forces of darkness that exist in the invisible realm around us. War in the physical world will never be resolved in the flesh, and so it continues to be a controversial subject. In the spiritual realm there is a continuous battle going on regardless of man's opinion.

The Spiritual Warrior is well-aware the spiritual realm does exist and is equipped to fight on another's behalf. The Holy Spirit lives within the Spiritual Warrior and so it is, he is trained to discern between the ways of God and the ways of the world of which

Satan rules.   Jesus knew Satan would use every enticement to lure man's heart away from God.

As a Spiritual Warrior you understand there are many souls who are unable to connect with their Heavenly Father. Without this connection the souls who reside on earth, in these last days, are unable to use the *Fruits of the Spirit* of which they are proficient in, as they have been unwillingly shackled to those things of the world around them. It will be up to the Spiritual Warriors to destroy what man does not understand; *who and what to fight against*. As such, there now are many *Earth Angels* scattered throughout the world who possess the fruits of the Father's Spirit who will light the way for those souls who have been cut off from the Divine.   *Earth Angels* are indeed Spiritual Warriors who possess spiritual realization so they can help others do the same, and in doing so bring an end to the suffering in the world.

CHAPTER 16
THE TRUTH REVEALED

While we have given you an overview of the weapons which you will use against Satan and his host of demons, it is crucial you understand the difference between an *Old Soul and an Earth Angel.* Our Heavenly Father knew there would come a time when even the most enlightened souls would have a difficult time accomplishing their earthbound mission. Jesus knew the weapons Satan was most proficient in and as such, knew there would come a time when *Earth Angels* would need to light the way for those souls who had been unduly restrained through no fault of their own. **Every soul who resides on earth, in these times, has chosen to do so. They knew they would be coming to earth in very challenging times. Although each soul would have a different agenda or goal they were to achieve, they would be hard pressed to understand the magnitude of what they would endure.** *Earth Angels* **were created specifically to serve the Heavenly Father. For this reason, they** possessed an inner strength and knowing that much of mortal man did not possess. They, as a result, possessed those traits which were of the Father, unlike the *Old Souls* who were seeking opportunities to help them become more fully enlightened in the ways of their beloved Father. These *Old Souls* would have various assignments according to their purpose. Some souls would become actively involved in what mankind would refer to as *"The Tribulation"*, while others would accomplish what their soul knew would be the last opportunity for them to take advantage of the School of Life on earth.

Whatever the case may be, our Father knew these *Earth Angels* would play a most important role in preparing the way for the Father's Kingdom to reign on earth. Jesus would do everything that was possible to ensure man was given every opportunity to understand what in this life was the reality and what was the illusion.

Satan, as the Mighty Deceiver, understood all one had to do was change one's perception of a situation that would create a new reality for mankind. If something is not real, then it is, in fact, an illusion. Webster defines illusion as: *a thing that is likely perceived by the senses, a false idea or belief.* All Satan had to do was use the senses man was most familiar with to create what man would accept as reality. Nothing could or would be farther from the truth!

Satan, as you can see, knew that in order to protect this illusion man must lose all connection to the Divine. For without the life thread that was necessary for the soul to accomplish his sole purpose, the soul would be all but lost to His Heavenly Father.

Jesus had promised He would never again destroy the earth as in the days of Noah. This time He and He alone would ensure there would be a **new world on the horizon** in which He would dominate. It will be at the appropriate time that Jesus will establish His Kingdom on earth as it is in heaven!

THE GREAT PLAN

CHAPTER 17
THE POWER OF PRAYER

THE LORD'S PRAYER

Our Father who art in heaven, hallowed be Thy name, Thy kingdom come, Your will be done, on earth as it is in heaven. Give us this day our daily bread and forgive us our trespass as we forgive those who trespass against us. Lead us not into temptation: but deliver us from evil. For Thine is the kingdom and the power and the glory, for ever and ever. Amen

Currently, there are a vast majority of people on earth who know of the Lord's Prayer. Yet, for far too long many have ceased to think about the meaning of these words. There are now several generations who do not even know what the Lord's Prayer is. This will prove to be of major concern for the United States of America. For a nation that was founded under God a most dangerous shift is transpiring in the country's foundational beliefs.

In years past, the Lord's Prayer had been recited in school along with the Pledge of Allegiance affirming the United States is one Nation under God. In 1963 prayer was officially banned from public schools. This ban was a result of atheists' pursuit to ban prayer in public schools and to enforce separation of church and state. This was the beginning of the outspoken minority affecting the silent majority. While seemingly innocent on the surface, this would alter the principles the United States had been founded on. This was just the beginning of one of the many subtle tactics Satan would use against Jesus' precious souls. Jesus knew it was the words within the Lord's Prayer that held the answers for what mankind would be seeking. For these very words held the key to what is to come for all of God's children. Jesus knew of the many events that would occur prior to His return. He knew firsthand what a formable adversary Lucifer and his legions were. There would be much that would transpire in the future that Jesus would use as a catalyst to awaken as many souls as possible. Jesus knew there was much that needed to be understood by His children. All must pay attention to the times for the battle between good and evil was intensifying. Evil has always existed, and this would be the final battle in which Satan and his legion of fallen angels would be exposed for what they were.

Jesus knew there were many throughout the earth who did not know Him. Many did not understand where the Kingdom of God could be found. Those who revered the Bible did not spend time in communion with their Heavenly Father and had not established a relationship with Him. As a result, they were unable to recognize or trust the still voice which came from within. While religion taught about Jesus and His Father's Kingdom, there were far too many who did not avail themselves of this wondrous relationship within. A Kingdom that was within for all who accepted Jesus Christ as their Savior. "Thy kingdom come, thy will be done on earth as it is in heaven", Jesus proclaimed.

Many did not pay attention to the words found within the Lord's Prayer nor take them in a literal sense. Until man embraces that which is of our Father's will, His kingdom will not reign on earth. Satan was well aware of mankind's weaknesses. He would keep man so distracted with the rigors of daily life that he would spend less and less time with the Divine and more and more time with the enticements the world had to offer. Complacency would play a major role in man's inability to foresee what was rooted in evil. For this reason, Jesus would allow certain events to occur, using these events as a wake-up call for mankind. These types of recent events would prove to be the catalyst which would help to prepare for His Kingdom on earth.

Thy will be done:

Our Father's ways are not the ways of this world. In order to embrace the will of our Heavenly Father one must desire His will above all else. As a result, one is not held captive by the standards of man. Standards which are predicated by man's ego and worldly ambitions. Those who embrace our Father's will turn inward for the guidance and answers they are seeking. They know He has their best and highest interest at heart, truly believing, *"Father does indeed know best"*. For this reason, they give thanks in all things embracing His will as their own. They know Jesus is sufficient unto all of their needs. In embracing our Father's will, there will be times you will not fully understand the reasons why or even the outcome, yet you must trust He is all knowing and as a result, right resolution will prevail. In responding to our Father's will, you will be led by His Spirit. You will exercise a higher wisdom assured in the knowledge you have been given. Man cannot fully understand that which he cannot accept; therefore, those who embrace our Father's will, truly will come to understand the ways of the Divine.

<u>Forgive Us Our Trespasses:</u>

"Forgive them Father for they know not what they do." These were the words Jesus spoke prior to His passing. Webster defines trespasses as: *an act of sin or offense, a violation of God's law or a wrong done to another person, often involving crossing a boundary of failing to meet God's standards.*

Jesus understood the **"human condition"** having experienced firsthand the choices one makes, as a result of free will. There were times these choices would unknowingly inflict pain on self or another. Jesus knew the true essence of life is to learn, to serve, and to grow. Often, these choices formed one's own lesson plan. Choices, if one could make over again, knowing what they knew now, would have been different. For this reason, our Father has always said, **"There is no such thing as a mistake for mistakes are merely a part of one's lesson plan. A lesson which once learned will enable one to share their newfound wisdom with others."**

Jesus knew the important thing was what one learned from each lesson. Satan thrived on the mistakes humans would make, insuring one would not learn their lesson, using tools of bitterness and anger to torment Jesus' precious souls. Jesus understood there would be those times when there would be those lessons that would cause one to seek forgiveness from one another. There would be those times they would seek forgiveness from the Heavenly Father as well.

Sowing seeds of bitterness would keep Jesus' precious souls from experiencing the love and peace which the act of forgiveness brings. Jesus knew an unforgiving spirit dwells in darkness opening the door for the adversary. Hate and anger thrive on an unforgiving spirit which creates a barrier to the Divine. Jesus knew through the spirit of forgiveness one would be able to learn from their mistakes. They then would share their lessons with one another, and as a result, a higher understanding would prevail. Forgiveness would therefore be a strong deterrent in the fight against evil.

Lead Us Not Into Temptation But Deliver Us From Evil:

Jesus understood the choices mankind would be faced with due to having free will. There would be many temptations on earth that mankind would be exposed to. The material world would use technology to distract man from seeking that which would nurture the soul, hence the primary reason for his existence on earth. Technology would prove to be a huge temptation for many. Jesus knew in the future man would spend countless hours on social networks searching for activity and entertainment one had not previously had exposure to. The computer would bring things into the home, which in years past man had not been tempted by. Via the fingertip, man was able to have a vast array of information at his fingertips. As a result, many would become involved with information and subject matter they had not been previously exposed to. Man would develop compulsive habits because of the hectic lifestyles they lived. Peace, as a result, was not easily found as many struggled to support the world he had created. Because of this, there would be many souls who would be tempted away from the Father almost as though He had never existed.

In the final battle between good and evil man would come to understand how evil had managed to enter the lives of many. The evil which had become ever present throughout the world would be difficult for man to comprehend. Jesus knew there would be many souls in the future who would be crying out on a daily basis. Man would look to man for the answers they sought and as a result, these answers would be counterpart to what would nurture the soul. Man would be held captive by more and more things, thereby distancing himself from the Divine. As foretold in the Lord's Prayer, *deliverance from evil in the end would come and the Father's Kingdom would reign on earth!*

<u>For Thine Is the Kingdom And The Power And The Glory:</u>

Our Father's Kingdom is universal over all of mankind and all things in the world. Our Father is the King of all Nations. It is His duty to defend and provide for man's welfare. Our Father has the power to give above our asking and understanding. The honor and glory of all will resound from God. This excellence is eternal and will last forever throughout eternity.

THE GREAT PLAN

CHAPTER 18
PRAYER WARRIORS
VERSUS
SPIRITUAL WARRIORS

Many times, you will hear about those who are called in earnest to actively participate as **Prayer Warriors**. These warriors are those who are dedicated to praying often for others or for specific situations. A Prayer Warrior uses prayer as a weapon and a means of intercession, seeking God's intervention in spiritual battle. A Prayer Warrior believes in the power of prayer and desires to stand in the gap between God and humanity. In conclusion, a Prayer Warrior consistently prays for the sick, those in need of the gospel and will often engage in extended periods of prayer and intercession. A Prayer Warrior is a type of Spiritual Warrior, but not all Spiritual Warriors are Prayer Warriors.

It is important to point out the differences between a *Spiritual Warrior* and a *Prayer Warrior*. A Spiritual Warrior engages in a broader range of spiritual practices, including prayer, discernment, seeking wisdom and actively combating spiritual darkness. He will actively seek to understand spiritual truths, resisting temptation and living a life that reflects their faith. He desires to live a life that honors God actively participating in the spiritual battle against evil.

<u>Benefits of Prayer:</u>

1. Prayer in general is important because it fosters a deeper connection with a Higher Power. Prayer can provide emotional support and can offer a sense of peace and guidance. Prayer enables one to communicate with a Higher Power, whether it is God or a Spiritual Force, that allows the individual to express one's thoughts, feelings, and needs.
2. When you engage in prayer it will strengthen one's faith and deepen your relationship with the Divine. This will provide a sense of connection and higher purpose that one finds in the world.
3. Prayer can be a way through the Holy Spirit to seek guidance, wisdom, and direction in the challenges of which one faces on earth. There is, after all, no question our Father will not answer. The more you seek, the more you will find!
4. Prayer provides an opportunity to express gratitude for our blessings and experiences which

fosters a sense of appreciation for the blessings we have received. *Prayer is the pause that refreshes,* for it takes us away from the daily rigors of life providing a sacred space for contemplation and emotional release.

5. In prayer one can experience a peace which defies human understanding helping one navigate the many challenges of life.

6. When one enters into communion with their Heavenly Father, they will discover that which is their purpose. This then will enable one to discover the true meaning of life fostering a connection to something much larger than themselves. Additionally, prayer is a fundamental practice in many religions.

Now, that we have listed the benefits of prayer, let us get down to the "nitty gritty", so to speak. Yes, the most important aspects or practical details.

Conversations with God:

It was Jesus who said to the disciples, ***"For I tell you it is for your good that I am going away. For if I do not go away the "Helper" will not come to you. But if I go, I will send Him to you."*** This Helper is none other than the Spirit of our loving God! It is the same Spirit who resides in the

Father, and the same Spirit who resides in Jesus. Our Father's Spirit resides in all who believe in Jesus Christ.

Our Heavenly Father knows all about you as well as the deepest desires of your heart. You have been created by our Heavenly Father. Our Father has said, ***"I am in you, and you are in Me. All that I am you are and all that I have you have."***

Our Father has known you since the very day you were created. His love is *unconditional* and as any Father would, He only wants what is in your best and highest interest.

Our Heavenly Father longs to have a relationship with you. Unlike any other on earth, He is available twenty-four hours a day seven days a week. Often, He will awaken you in the still of the night as there are not the distractions which can occupy your mind throughout the day (*In the still of the night when you cannot but sleep, God is tapping at the window of your soul! - ABBA and Company*).

There is no right or wrong way to pray, yet, Jesus' children believe they need to recite fanciful prayers that have been created by someone else. This is not necessary to engage in a conversation with Jesus. It is possible to enter into a two-way conversation with the Spirit of the living God. First and foremost, you must be still and know that He is God. You must believe in this reality. In the beginning, His voice may seem unfamiliar to you for it is a voice you cannot hear with your physical ears, but rather a voice that comes from the center of your being. For this is where the Holy Spirit resides. <u>The only condition to His Spirit residing within is that you must extend an invitation to enter. For He will not go where He is not welcome. When you acknowledge your belief in the Holy Spirit this will be the beginning of a most wonderful relationship.</u>

Often, when one prays there will be thoughts which enter in from one's conscious mind interrupting their ability to feel His presence. The Holy Spirit is always available and so it is, you must learn to exercise your spiritual ears. There is no question He will not answer. Many times, you may think He does not hear you because the answer is not what you have been praying for.

This can be very difficult for Jesus's children to understand. Often, one prays for answers that would only act as a band aid, never getting to that which is the solution; the root cause of what one is praying for. So many people claim their prayers have gone unanswered, yet in truth, they have not prayed for what would be the ultimate solution. The Holy Spirit will help you to understand what is the heart of the matter. That which will result in right resolution or that which is in the highest and best interest of one's soul! When you pray and doubt the outcome of your prayer, in essence, you are doubting God.

"Jesus never desired for the church to take the place of your ability to communicate with Me. Effective communication must work both ways. There must be an exchange of information such as ideas, feelings, speech, writing and signals." -Holy Spirit

Satan, the Mighty Deceiver, has done an excellent job of keeping man from understanding their true, identity and that they have access to the spiritual world. As in any relationship, the more time one spends in this wondrous relationship the stronger the relationship will become.

The challenge in the beginning is to be able to distinguish what is from God. This will always be your highest thought and the strongest feeling. To truly know God in a personal way, one must be willing to stop telling themself they already know Him. To know Him and of Him are two different things entirely. To do so, you must change the way you view earthly experiences. You cannot change the outer experience, and so it is, you must change the inner experience. When you open the door to this most wonderful relationship you will soon experience that which has kept you from conversing with our Heavenly Father.

THE GREAT PLAN

CHAPTER 19
THE ROLE THE PROPHET WILL PLAY IN OUR FATHER'S GREAT PLAN

Jesus knew there would come a time when prophets would play an important role in the fight against evil. Just as in the time of Moses, prophets would be used in modern day times to alert Jesus' precious souls of what was looming in the future. Satan, however, had convinced many Christians that prophets were nonexistent in the world today. Of course, prophets have always existed. Satan, understanding full well the role of the prophet, had done his utmost to steer the church away from prophets, warning clergy and parishioners to be aware of false prophets in the last days. For he knew the prophets would expose the many weapons he and his demons would use to destroy God's people. One must understand the role of a prophet is a call directly from God or a Divine entity to deliver messages or prophecies. Prophets often receive insights from a Higher Power. Wendy and Jillian were aware of the various prophets throughout the world. Social media made it possible for various prophets to share what God had revealed to each. Some prophets would attach a specific timeline or date to that which they received, yet most true prophets steered away from doing so.

Jesus looked to prophets and *Earth Angels* to share God's messages with the world. Let us examine the *"**Traits of Prophets**"*. This will help to give some much-needed clarification to this most important role. The characteristics of a prophet are, in some ways, the same as a Spiritual Warrior as they stand the gap between that which is of the material and that which is spiritual.

1. A prophet is seen as someone who speaks the truth, especially concerning justice and spiritual truths and acts as an intercessor seeking God's will and guidance for others, while demonstrating a Christlike character.
2. Prophets expose the lies of the Mighty Deceiver. They need to express their thoughts and ideas verbally, especially in the areas of right and wrong.
3. Prophets do not hesitate to share their own personal faults in hopes others would do the same about theirs. They are loyal to truth even if it involves cutting off relationships, if

necessary, in these last days in order to expose the truth and the magnitude of evil mankind would now be facing.

4. Prophets would be called to open the eyes of as many people as possible in order to stand strong against the weapons Satan was now using in full force against the many unsuspecting souls of the world.

There would be many now who would turn to the prophets for direction and answers that they would not receive from the clergy. As a result, prophets would play a major role in the fight against evil.

THE GREAT PLAN

CHAPTER 20
FROM AFAR

The Angels in Heaven were on high alert now as they could see time was of the essence. Everything that could be done to get the attention of the humans who resided on earth, must be done. This would not prove to be an easy task as there were so many distractions in the world. Far too many had lost sight of what was the reality and what was the illusion. The angels knew things on earth were heating up and they would get far worse before they would get better. They understood the magnitude of evil that had been unleashed throughout the world.

Although Jesus assured evil in the end would be overthrown, there were many in the heavens who were becoming anxious as to when this final battle would take place. So much had happened because of the evil that had permeated the souls of so very many on earth. There was still hope more souls would be saved even as Satan and his legion of demons were now raising havoc in every corner of the world.

St. Michael and his legion of warriors had been working fervently to keep Satan's legion at bay. Not only were they fighting against those in the Heavenly realm, they were now in battle with the demons who roamed throughout the world.

Oh, if only mankind understood the reality of such Spiritual Beings. It was impossible to fight against that which you do not believe exists, let alone the weapons they would use.

There were rumors Jesus was preparing to take the next step in His plan to save as many souls from the wiles of Satan as possible. Although the exact details were unknown, they would be extremely important in the final battle between good and evil.

Prayers were being sent out daily with a sense of urgency that had not been seen since the annihilation of the Jewish people of World War Two. Many, once again, felt so hopeless and as a result had drawn farther and farther away from the Divine.

All in the heavens were most anxious for what was soon to come. They knew how crucial it was for the Lord's children to be able to commune with their

Heavenly Father. For without this ability many would be in danger of losing their way.

Those in the Heavens knew there was much looming in the not-too-distant future giving thanks for the many *Earth Angels* who were now scattered throughout the world. It was a relief to all in the heavens that Jesus was ready to implement the next step in His plan, which was to overthrow the magnitude of evil that Satan had unleashed in full force against the world. Jesus had been patient for so long and even now He still longed to save as many souls as possible.

The love Jesus has for His children is beyond the scope of human understanding. He knew time was running out. Something needed to be done to awaken His children. All needed to understand the reality of the times they were living in. There were so many signs that had already come to pass, yet many still refused to pay attention to what was looming on the horizon.

Jesus currently had His *Earth Angels* scattered throughout the world. In addition, there were many prophets alerting man to what was looming on the horizon and the importance of fighting against the forces of evil hell bent on destroying God's precious souls.

Jesus was currently weaving an invisible thread, connecting those of like minds and spirits, through the Holy Spirit. Soon, much would be revealed and once they were, things would move very quickly throughout the world.

Satan had done his work well and placed his legion of demons strategically throughout the world, for the battle would soon be apparent for all to see. St. Michael and his legion were standing guard as all in his legion were prepared to protect Jesus' chosen from the onslaught of evil, which was soon to be unleashed. Fear would run rampant amongst humans as none could ever have conceived events, which had been foretold to take place, were now happening!

Soon, Jesus would make Himself known to all of mankind as the breath of the Holy Spirit would descend upon all those inhabiting the earth. All who resided in heaven had been told by the Father what this would entail. Those who resided on earth would be enveloped by the Holy Spirit. It would be as if each was surrounded by a dense fog, a fog so thick that nothing could penetrate its walls. For the chosen, this will be as though they have returned to the womb as this is when they will understand from where they have come. This will be when they would know that which is the reality and that which is an illusion. Each will see the effects of the choices they had made throughout their lives. For many this will be a difficult encounter. Many will see how their actions and inactions have affected those who are a part of their earthly life. This unveiling of the Holy Spirit will reveal much that has been untold in the world to date. This _awakening or warning_ will be the catalyst that will ignite many souls. Souls which had come dangerously close to being consumed by the spirit of darkness. These souls who will embrace that which is of the Divine will, now, will be guided by the light and a new understanding will abound.

Even though all would experience this revelation, many would relish a scientific explanation for what they had encountered. Many would embrace an alternative answer for what was the supernatural. They will seek answers that would allow them to exercise their own free will. A free will that would reject that of the Divine.

Wendy and Jillian, having experienced the human condition, understood how and why Jesus' timing was so important. Once man understood that which was the reality, it would require him to be immersed in the Holy Spirit, as this reality could be most startling to those who had based their faith on an illusion, which, after all, was relative to the human condition. A condition that relied on things of the exterior for survival and that which mortal man has professed to be true. Human emotions reacted to outside stimuli creating barriers to a peace which escapes human understanding. The human condition is simply a condition the soul had agreed to, albeit a temporary condition at best. When the veil is lifted the soul is ready to assume its rightful position as a Spiritual Being. Initially, this is difficult for those who have been held hostage by those things of the world provoking initial feelings of fear, unrest and anger.

One must understand why the veil had remained, even for those who followed the teachings of Jesus Christ. What these teachings *did not include* was, of course, the importance of all souls being enrolled in The School of Life, let alone that it even existed. As a result, there would be much that would not be revealed until the appropriate time.

Once the veil was lifted there would be those who felt deceived. This is a result of what they had been conditioned to believe was the truth. For much of what man had learned was based on what one could see through their mortal eyes and that which was of his external environment. For man, much of what he saw was his reality. To think all one had experienced while on earth was but an illusion was very difficult to comprehend.

Since all souls had signed an original contract prior to arriving on earth, they of course, did not remember what had taken place prior to their arrival, let alone the conditions they had previously agreed to.

Jesus knew timing was crucial because once the veil was lifted every soul would need to have time to reacquaint themselves with those truths that the Father had now shared, were in fact, the reality. He knew there would be an adjustment period needed for one to understand they were not human beings, but rather, Spiritual Beings who must now transition from that which was of the physical to that of a Spiritual

Being. One must now be willing to die unto self and embrace the ideals of the Heavenly Father. These would, in the end, be the very weapons that would defeat the enemy. As you can imagine, if this was a stretch for an *Earth Angel* who had been experiencing the human condition, how difficult would it be for those souls who had lost their ability to connect with the Divine?

Because things were ramping up on earth to a frenzied state, Jesus now found it necessary to indoctrinate His chosen souls to the truths, which would enable them to stand strong against the enemy. He understood that while many had been called, in the end, few would be chosen. These few would indeed become an active participant in Jesus' Supreme Army. For this reason, all must come together sharing the Spiritual Gifts they had been given.

Old Souls who had been previously stuck, unable to express the very ideals they had learned, were no longer held captive by the enemy. These are the ones who would now awaken as if from a *"deep sleep"*. Jesus would use that which man would label as supernatural for all to witness as there could be no other explanation for it. Yet, there would be those who would refuse to understand the meaning of the times and the existence of our Heavenly Father. So, you can understand why the veil had to be lifted for this would not be a battle that could be won in the flesh but one that would take the strength of Spiritual Beings. One could safely say it would take *all hands-on-deck* serving in the highest capacity, utilizing the weapons they were highly skilled in. This training would be far superior to that which mortal man could understand.

THE GREAT PLAN

CHAPTER 21
THE TRANSITION

The souls who inhabit the earth are Citizens of Heaven who, in essence, are Spiritual Beings. The initial transition from the spiritual to the physical does not happen instantaneously. There is a period of nine months in which the soul becomes adjusted to the physical condition. Once the soul arrives on earth all attention is relegated to the physical. In the beginning, the soul is still very connected to his Heavenly Father. He is assigned a guardian angel to escort him on his earthly journey. Many times, the young human can be heard talking to what some would define as an *imaginary friend*. As the name implies it is not real and therefore, does not exist. Yet, to the young adolescent this imaginary friend is very real and very much a part of their existence. As time passes, he is unduly convinced by those around him it is indeed a figment of his imagination. As a result, he then begins to direct his attention to what can be seen by the mortal eye. He depends on his physical senses to satiate the needs of the flesh paying little or no attention to the most important part of his being, the soul.

Religion, which once provided a window for spiritual awareness in the current world, has become undesirable for most humans, thereby creating barriers to what is the very life thread of the soul. Mankind would have no idea of what he was truly capable of as a Spiritual Being. Although many had stated man was indeed capable of far more than he realized, very few believed in this reality. For man behaved in accordance to what he believed to be true.

"Jesus Christ is the Ambassador of Truth" must now be the motto to awaken those souls in mankind which had been sorely neglected. Man would now require a much-needed reality check. One that would persuade man to acknowledge the still voice from within. Jesus would now use all to His Supreme advantage. He would use that which encouraged dis-ease and unrest to open the door to a new understanding. As man becomes less and less enamored with the things of the exterior, he would

begin to question that which he had not questioned before. What once had provided a sense of security seemed far removed in a world filled with chaos and confusion. As a result, man would begin to look elsewhere for the answers he was seeking. He would direct his attention to that which was of the interior, rather than, a world full of conflict and dis-ease. He would now respond to the still voice of his soul who understood he was a Spiritual Being called to a higher purpose!

THE GREAT PLAN

CHAPTER 22
THE REALITY

In these last days, the reality would be ***"There will be many who are called and yet, few will be chosen"***. This is not what our Father intended for any of His precious souls, and as such, He understood there would come a precise time when He would allow this magnitude of evil to be exposed as never before. An evil of which most of mankind would be hard pressed to believe existed, let alone who and what was responsible for the overall state of mankind. Mankind would soon be at a most critical point in his earthly journey. The decisions every soul would face would now be at the mercy of the human condition each found themselves in. The decisions that would be made would have a permanent and lasting effect throughout eternity. Those who were able to pass the test of time will endure until the end. **Jesus knew Satan would use the conscious mind of man whenever possible to create barriers to the truth; that which is the reality. There will be those who are actively engaged in the battle between good**

126

and evil who are Divinely guided. Spiritual Warriors, Prayer Warriors, Earth Angels, Prophets and Old Souls would need to come together combining those spiritual gifts and talents, which in the end would defeat the enemy. In order for this to transpire, mankind must be able to see the evil that had spread its tentacles throughout the world.

Jesus would allow incidences to occur in hopes man would no longer turn a blind eye to what, at one time, would have seemed morally wrong and inhumane. Because many souls had lost their connection to their Heavenly Father, they were dominated by that which was geared towards the physical aspect of one's being. This would ensure man look outside of himself to fulfill those needs of the flesh, having little if nothing to do with the most important part of one's being. It would therefore be, as though the Spiritual Being was nonexistent leaving the soul to flounder in the darkness.

When the soul is separated from the joy of our Heavenly Father it is as though the soul is in hell. The ultimate goal, while on earth, is for the soul to be able to fully express itself while in the human body. Yes, to achieve that which he is destined to fulfill.

THE GREAT PLAN

CHAPTER 23
THE TRUMPET SOUNDS

Before we begin, one must understand the role of the trumpet as referred to in the Bible. In the Bible trumpets played a crucial role in signaling alarms, gathering the people, and marking Holy days, while also foreshadowing events of the end times, including the rapture and judgments.   The trumpets in Revelation are seen as a call for God's people to remember, repent, and anticipate the return of the Lord.

As you can see the role of the trumpet is most important in the battle between good and evil. Jesus was about to introduce a very important part of His plan. He would need to find the appropriate person who would fulfill the role of the Trumpeter. One who would alert all to a magnitude of evil such as mankind would not think possible in the world today.

Satan, who had dominion over the earth, was well-versed in all that was of the ego. He knew the ego was primarily concerned with self and selfish interests. Interests that would keep one occupied with material wealth, prestige, and control. The ego would keep man so preoccupied with material things of the world he would have little or no interest in spiritual matters or even God for that matter. As long as the ego was the dominant force, mankind would be lulled into a false sense of reality. Of course, this was a major objective of Satan and his legion to keep man from acknowledging he was created in his Father's image and as such, was capable of far more than what he as a human understood. Although he was experiencing the human condition, he was a Citizen of Heaven temporarily residing on earth. He was, in fact, one of Jesus' precious souls, a Spiritual Being who would help prepare the way for our Father's Kingdom to reign on earth.

When Jesus met with the Senior Angels in heaven, He told them who He would choose to alert all to the magnitude of evil throughout the world. This would need to be someone who was most familiar with the very weapons Satan would use against Jesus' precious souls. It would need to be someone who was most familiar with the traits of the ego and the wiles of the devil.

As in the case of the ego, it is of course, a double edge sword. The positive traits of the ego are; confidence, resiliency, management of emotions effectively, problem solvers, adaptable to changing situations, honest, strong morals, understands one's strengths and weaknesses and assertive. The negative traits of the ego are; reacts negatively to criticism, arrogant, believes himself superior to others, uses others for personal goals and quick to blame and judge others. As you can see the ego is indeed a double edge sword.

When selecting the appropriate person to confront the wiles of Satan one must familiarize themselves with the deceptive tactics used by Satan to ensnare or harm people, often through *temptation, doubt, and fear.*

Jesus knew of such a man as He had been observing him for quite some time. Long before his arrival on earth, Jesus knew the ideals this soul had acquired and those that were lacking. The Spiritual Gifts he would be given must serve him well in the assignment he would be called to accomplish. It would prove to be a most difficult assignment indeed. This person would be given the **Spiritual Gift of**

Wisdom (*of understanding what is true and what is right*). This gift would be a powerful weapon against the Mighty Deceiver.

And so it was, there was **Donald Trump** who would expose the magnitude of evil that encompassed every corner of the earth. All, in the counsel, agreed that upon reviewing the traits Donald Trump possessed, that he was indeed the right man for the job.

Wendy and Jillian intrinsically knew when Donald Trump was elected President, he was chosen by the Father to expose the magnitude of evil within the United State and throughout the world. In working for the Heavenly Father, they knew the Father's ways were not the ways of the world. There were a great many who were up in arms at Trump being elected President, as he portrayed characteristics that were viewed as the negative aspects of one's ego. As a result, he was known for his quick tongue and ill-mannered responses leaving a sour taste in the mouths of many.

These initial four years would act as a training ground for that which he would need in the years that followed. Trump, never having been a politician, was introduced to a great deal he had not been exposed to in the world he had previously amassed for himself. None the less, the four years he was in office had allowed him a great deal to be accomplished. The economy had never been better and the country was experiencing a security they had not experienced in quite some time. Incredible as it may seem, he was not reelected for a second term. The Mighty Deceiver struck a mighty blow opening the door to an implosion of evil the United States had never deemed possible.

Wendy and Jillian were well versed in the ways of our Heavenly Father. Yet, nothing could have prepared them for the turn of events that would open the door for evil to change the moral fiber of a nation. Change in ways that had not been altered since the days of Sodom and Gomorrah. Even as Earth Angels, Wendy and Jillian could not believe Trump would not be reelected as up until the last moment it appeared he had won by a landslide.

One must remember Jesus does not cause bad things to happen but will allow them for His Supreme advantage. Even though the Father knew Trump was uncovering some of the corruption within the government, He knew there was a magnitude of evil lurking beneath the surface that would play havoc with the one Nation founded under God with liberty and justice for all.

Jesus knew the enemy now had the opportunity to implement his evil agenda. Those who had been complacent in the past would soon see, with their mortal eyes, that which they had turned a blind eye to.

CHAPTER 24
HELL ON EARTH

There is no other way to describe what the ensuing four years would entail. One would be hard pressed to believe the sins of Sodom and Gomorrah would now become awe apparent in the twentieth century. Murder, theft, adultery, abuse of power, prideful and mocking behavior. In addition, sexual violence and trafficking, and abuse as well as homosexuality and perversion would run rampant. A country that had once been founded on Godly principles would now become overrun with a level of sin infesting the very moral fiber of mankind. These sins would now be used to change the very culture of a nation. The Ten Commandments for many would now become Commandments that were no longer revered by the masses.

One may ask, *"Why would someone want to destroy a nation that was initially founded as One Nation Under God?"* The short answer is Satan was hell bent on destroying God's precious souls. Satan would use people, places, and things to captivate the heart, mind, and soul of mankind. He knew in the end, mankind, would eventually destroy itself. All he needed to do was change man's perception regarding the very ideals of the Heavenly Father.

Jesus knew there would soon come a time when one would not be able to find that which was the truth. The Mighty Deceiver had altered the truth to form a new reality; one that would enable his sinful ways to replace Godly virtues and principles.

One Nation under God in the next four years would become divided. This division would ensure unrest, and hatred would become present throughout society. Man would begin to see signs that the Heavenly Father said would become increasingly apparent closer to Jesus' return. There were far too many souls who were dangerously close to losing their way, and so, the Lord would use those situations that were of the enemy to awaken all to reality.

Never had such a magnitude of deception existed within the Government of the people, by the people and for the people. Biden, who was the acting President of the United States, was overseeing the Nation, yet was not the one calling the shots. In the latter two years of his Presidency, it would become apparent he was operating at half mast, displaying signs of dementia for all to see (Webster defines demented as: *behaving wildly, irrationally on account of anger, distress, excitement).* In the case of Biden, it became increasingly apparent an evil presence had infiltrated the very core of the United States Government. An evil which was now becoming more and more apparent to those who were filled with the Holy Spirit; those who would use their spiritual ears and eyes to see the truth! There were many who were beginning to question those who held leadership roles within the government, and so it was, the wheels would now be set in motion for God's Supreme Army to play an active role in the weeks and months ahead!

THE GREAT PLAN

CHAPTER 25
THE BATTLE INTENSIFIES

Jesus' Great Plan was going exactly as He had intended. Every detail was being tended to. Details which would lull the Mighty Deceiver into a false sense of security. Jesus would allow situations that would give Satan and his legion enough rope in which to hang themselves. A rope, that in the end, would put a noose around Satan's neck once and for all.

Jesus had used the four years of which Biden was President as an opportunity to fine tune those traits of which Donald Trump would need to become more proficient in. Those traits which in the past had been sorely lacking, and as such, left a bad impression on a great many whom he would now need to convince he was the best man for the job.

Experience was the best teacher. Jesus knew the many emotions Trump would experience in the four years of Biden's Presidency. Emotions that he would learn to keep in check. He would need to learn to respond to that which was of the Father. **Humility is the cornerstone on which all great works are**

accomplished. **True humility enables one to respond in a manner that promotes good will, rather than that which feeds the beast. Trump would learn to exercise his higher consciousness. That which is one with the mind of Christ. Jesus knew what Trump was destined to complete, and would ensure he had all at his disposal as he needed it.**

This molding and shaping for Trump would be crucial as there was much at stake for the future of the United States as well as Nations throughout the world. Humility would ensure one's obedience to God, respect for oneself and others, submissiveness and modesty while exercising the importance of not viewing oneself as greater than God, but as His obedient servant.

Humility involves recognizing one's own limitations and dependence on God, rather than relying on self-sufficiency or a prideful nature. Humility is a key characteristic of God's people and service to others.

Many would begin to compare Donald Trump to King David in the Bible who acknowledged his own sin and sought God's forgiveness, showing humility in his repentance. Jesus knew humility would enable Trump to foster healthy relationships by promoting empathy, understanding, and a willingness to listen to others.

And so, it was these four years that would ensure the necessary changes would occur within the recesses of Trump's being. He would establish a deep and abiding relationship with the Holy Spirit. A relationship of which he would come to depend on in the ensuing battle between good and evil. A battle in which Trump would begin to understand, was not of the flesh but between principalities!

THE GREAT PLAN

CHAPTER 26
GATHERING OF HIS FLOCK

This would be a battle of which *"to whom much is given much would be required"*. All who would be called to *active duty* must now operate at the highest capacity. While Donald Trump would be victorious in securing another four years as President there would be much that would need to be brought to the attention of the masses. What Trump would tend to would prepare the way for Jesus' Kingdom to reign on earth. Jesus would use information that Trump uncovered as a way to address what lay beneath the surface. What was of the world, man would soon discover, was sorely lacking as events would soon spiral out of control. Wars and rumors of wars would escalate. The wealth of many Nations would become severely compromised as each struggled to secure its economic future. Division would not only be limited to one's own country, but would intensify between Nations that once were unified. The political arena would spew a hatred, which would only intensify as evil was now running rampant throughout the world.

THE GREAT PLAN

St. Michael and his legion were on high alert as they witnessed the evil that was imploding throughout the United States. Alliances, the United States had at one time depended on, were feeling the effects of the evil that would be hard to overthrow. Nations would now rise up against Nations, and Kingdom against Kingdom. There would be famines and earthquakes in various places. He knew many would turn away from their faith and would betray and hate each other. Because of the increase in wickedness, the love of most would grow cold.

For these reasons, St. Michael and his legion were on high alert for they knew this was the beginning of the end for those who refused to acknowledge the signs of the time. Soon, very soon, he knew man would be forced to take a stand. It would be for mankind the biggest decision one would ever make. For all this would be a decision they never saw coming.

Wendy and Jillian knew the time had come when much would be revealed. That which was unknown before would now be allowed as Jesus, the Ambassador of Truth, would divulge information that one would be hard pressed to accept. Even those who could see with their mortal eyes what was transpiring throughout the world, would refuse to accept what was the reality. These are the ones who would hold fast to what they knew to be true, and that many would soon discover was but an illusion.

While one could understand why man would have a difficult time letting go of all they had been taught and believed to be true, since birth, there were those on the other hand who had a relationship with the Holy Spirit who understood the reality of what was now being revealed. These were the ones who would exercise their spiritual senses, letting go of all that was of the human condition.

Many times, Jesus had said, ***"There would come a time when mankind would have to make the most important choice of their lives***." Simply put, the choice would be to either move forward embracing this newfound reality or be left behind. Those who embraced this reality would no longer be tied to that which was of the world. Mankind would now pay little if no interest to those things which had once captured their attention, and what they had built their world around.

Satan, on the other hand, would do his best to generate fear among those whose faith was sorely lacking. These would be the souls who would be persuaded to follow and trust non-other than the *Antichrist. Many would be convinced he was the true savior, a deception so well executed many would not recognize he had not come to save but to destroy!*

PART 3

THE GREAT PLAN

CHAPTER 27
THINGS ARE HEATING UP!

Things on earth were heating up, such as never before! When I say heating up, one means literally. The magnitude of evil had reached a boiling point that would test mankind far beyond that which he thought could ever be humanly possible. The world as man had known it, since the great flood, was now being changed in ways one would never have believed possible let alone probable.

There are many reasons why things have reached such a feverish pitch as far too many humans had lost touch with reality. So many souls had lost their way and it would take an act of God to save these precious souls. Souls of which the Father had so desperately tried to awaken.

Even though the Heavenly Father had removed the veil for mankind to see the reality of what was transpiring, there were still far too many who refused to acknowledge what had been revealed. The Mighty Deceiver had succeeded in turning the hearts of man cold and so it was *"many had been called but very few had been chosen"*.

There were those, of course, who revered the Heavenly Father and had ceased to view the world through their mortal eyes but now viewed through that which was of their true nature; *that of a Spiritual Being.* What mankind was now witnessing would be a time of trial that many had never deemed possible.

Wendy and Jillian were sensing an urgency they had not felt before. Jesus had told them, **"They would know when the time was right?"** Yet, they could not help but wonder if the book would be completed soon enough. Wendy knew Jesus' timing was perfect. She prayed the book would be out in time to help all understand the reality.

Both Wendy and Jillian knew there were now countless souls who were in jeopardy of losing their way. Far too many souls would be unable to find their way back home. A home of which they once knew and no longer felt a connection to.

CHAPTER 28
THE PLAN AS REVEALED
IN THE BOOK OF REVELATION

Many biblical scholars had often referred to the *Book of Revelation* found within the Bible. This foretold of events and signs to come prior to Jesus' return to earth. All who worked for the Father were now being called to do their part in preparing the way for His Kingdom to reign on earth. Although there were those who were somewhat familiar with the signs that would be prevalent prior to His return, many refused to believe this would happen in their lifetime. For hadn't mankind been anticipating such a return for well over 2000 years?

Because there were many who would not refer nor understand the *Book of Revelation*, Jesus knew it was crucial the **"The Great Plan"** be written in a way for all to see and comprehend. Yes, in a way in which modern man could truly understand!

It was never Jesus' intention to keep His precious souls in the dark about what was to come. You must remember the *Book of Revelation* was written at a time when words and symbols took on a different meaning based on the current culture at that time. So, no wonder there were many who did not acknowledge the times they were living in. Nor, in truth, understand the reality. ***The Book of Revelation in the Bible was intended to be a symbolic and prophetic text that described God's plan for the end times emphasizing Jesus' ultimate victory and creation of a new Heaven and Earth.***

Revelation, as written in the Bible, anticipates Jesus' return as the ultimate King who, in the end, will defeat evil and establish His Kingdom on The Earth. It also depicts God's judgment on those who reject Him and His plans, as well as the triumph of believers. The *Book of Revelation*, despite the imagery of judgment and tribulation, offers hope for a new heaven and a new earth.

CHAPTER 29
EXTREME PLAN
VS
SUPREME PLAN

Jesus would use Divine Inspiration to guide His chosen *Earth Angels* as they moved ever closer to the mission they were destined to complete. When Wendy and Jillian reflected on the thirty plus years, since the forming of ABBA and Company, they could see how Jesus had been guiding them to this very point in time. A time when they would be responsible for sharing **Jesus' Great Plan** with the world. This plan would reveal the reality to all. Timing was crucial, for this book would provide many with the answers to questions they would unknowingly and desperately be seeking.

Even though Wendy and Jillian were *Angels on Assignment* they too would need to experience, firsthand, the magnitude of evil that had increased since they had arrived on earth. Not to mention, both had experienced firsthand the trappings of the ego and how Satan had successfully used it to keep mankind securely tethered to the world. His plan would ensure that man approached life from the outside in, having little if no interest in that which was of the Father's Kingdom.

Free will would be the catalyst that would be responsible for the choices mankind would make in the not-too-distant future. A will that for each would determine the fate of every soul who had chosen to be on earth and help prepare the world for a new beginning. What was to transpire in the months ahead would awaken those souls who had laid dormant in their human condition. A condition where most had lost interest in that which was of the spiritual.

In preparation for what was to come, the Heavenly Father had allowed the *Corona Virus* as a wake-up call for His beloved souls. You must remember our Father's ways are not the ways of the world. His wisdom goes well beyond the depth of what mankind comprehends. What is about to be shared is a profound example of the wisdom of our Heavenly Father.

Almost five years had passed since the *Corona Virus* had imploded upon the world. An implosion modern man had never experienced. For the first time in many years, the United States would experience a sudden collapse that would allow fear to run rampant amongst the masses. Fear would be the mighty weapon that caused mankind to react to the wiles of the adversary; to the wiles of Satan and his legion.

Man would be hard pressed to believe this virus, which was responsible for killing millions of people throughout the world, was created by one whose primary design was to control the world. A world that would be run by darkness and could ultimately destroy all who would not succumb to the agenda of the evil one. Yes, to that which was a part of Satan's "**extreme plan**".

The *Corona Virus* accomplished far more than what one would have thought humanly possible in the twentieth century. Almost every sector of public life was no longer allowed. Whenever possible, man was required to curtail all social activities which included public attendance in places of worship. Those employees who could work from home were mandated to do so as well. Students were also unable to attend public schools. Anything that would encourage people to gather was prohibited. The government exercised control over much of the population.

The medical community was desperate for that which would cure if not prevent the virus from ravaging the masses. The pharmaceutical companies were working tirelessly to produce a vaccine that would protect one from the virus, let alone, that which could save the lives of those who were already infected.

Wendy and Jillian could see the fear that was spreading like a cancer throughout the world. Fear would test the faith of the young and old alike. Many would now look to the world for the answers they would be seeking. Satan had all but shut down the world as he proceeded with the next part of his **"extreme plan"**.

This plan would ensure division would increase in a nation that had been founded upon *One Nation Under God*. If his plan succeeded it would never again be *One Nation Under God With Liberty and Justice*

For All. This division would not only affect the masses it would also create a wedge between family and friends.

They saw how the general public responded to the newly developed vaccine. One that had not been fully tested for potential side effects. Yet, this vaccine would become a mandatory requirement for many places of business and those in the medical community.

Even as *Earth Angels*, there were so many questions Wendy and Jillian had. One must remember they too were a part of the "human condition". A condition each knew they had to guard against. They were more than familiar with the weapons Satan would use, yet it never ceased to amaze them how easily man could be deceived. Oh, if only mankind understood the battle all souls were immersed in. A battle that most of man did not understand let alone acknowledge.

Chaos and confusion were powerful weapons Satan would use to create barriers to man going to the Kingdom within. For this is where man would find the answers to questions which mortal man could not. This is where they could find the truth and not the lies of the Mighty Deceiver. For it is through the Holy Spirit one can discover what lies beneath the surface, that which is hidden beneath the surface.

Wendy and Jillian knew this pandemic was just a preview of events yet to come. Additionally, each knew the world man had become familiar with would soon shift in ways most would not conceive of. They knew there was a spiritual movement that most of humanity was not able to grasp. As a result, many did not listen to that which their soul was prompting them to uncover. Far too many throughout the world did not understand they were not the sum-total of the physical condition of which they identified with.

In order for man to find *one's true self* they knew they must seek the truth. Yes, one must be willing to embrace that which is the reality. It was never intended for man to not understand the full magnitude of his being. Far too many were not willing to turn to the Kingdom within for the answers they would need. Jesus knew if man would but turn to the Kingdom within, he would find there were not the distractions one finds in the world. This is where he would discover the reality

What one spends his time on is what he will become. It will define who he is and what he identifies with. In the world today far too many of the Father's children do not acknowledge the existence of the soul. Until one acknowledges the soul's existence, they will not discover that which Satan has managed to keep hidden from much of mankind. Satan knew until the soul was acknowledged, the reality of who and what one is capable of would not become apparent. Wendy and Jillian knew that until man acknowledged they were, in essence, a Spiritual Being they would be held hostage by the world. They knew those who continued to seek within would find the world would subsequently be less of an enticement and as such, would automatically turn their interests elsewhere. Being *Earth Angels*, they understood this is the way it should be for this is how things will manifest when His Kingdom reigns on earth. To uncover that which is of the Father's Spirit, one must be willing to turn to the Kingdom within. One then cannot discover what they do not explore.

Jesus explained the purpose of the pandemic was used by the enemy as a catalyst to generate division amongst the masses as fear now overrode faith. When fear is present Wendy knew humans became putty in the hands of the enemy. When this occurs, many would agree to anything that would override the fear they had become saturated with. Once this happens the enemy has one eating out of the palm of his hands. When the vaccine became available, many were forced to make a choice that required those, who were one with the Father's Spirit, to take a stand. A stand one thought they would never be forced to make. Those who held fast to the Holy Spirit would be led by His spirit and would not fall victim to such a vaccine. This alone would separate the true believers from those whose faith was overrun by fear.

Currently, the recent tariffs which the United States was enforcing, were now generating the same type of chaos, confusion and yes, fear. Wendy and Jillian knew these tariffs were being used by the enemy to keep all so distracted they would not expect what was being masterminded by the enemy. The United States was being used by the enemy in ways much of man could not know. These tariffs would affect many Nations throughout the world.

Soon the world would change dramatically as alliances would now shift, resulting in new alliances forming. Man would find himself at a crossroads where he would be forced to make the most important choice/decision of his life. Those who would embrace the Father's will would move forward leaving behind all that did not or would not exist in the Father's Kingdom.

Satan, as part of his **extreme plan,** was hell bent on forming a "**New World Order**". One in which the *Antichrist* would present himself as the one who would save mankind from total annihilation. A world in which all would be controlled by a force so evil it would be difficult for many to believe such an evil did exist.

Not long after the tariffs would be put into effect, Wendy and Jillian had been told there would be a darkness that would encompass the world. This darkness would be experienced by all simultaneously. A darkness that will be initiated by Satan. This darkness will ensure communication and technology would no longer be available. Man, at this point, will once again react in much the same way as he did to the *Corona Virus* as much of man's activities were controlled in ways one never expected. The *Corona*

Virus was but a practice run initiated by the enemy to see how receptive mankind would be when forced to make a choice that would affect the destiny of each and every soul. The darkness which would implode upon the world would make the *Corona Virus* seem like child's play by comparison.

Now in the year 2025 fear would, once again, be the motivator for the choices mankind would make in the future. Once technology is no longer available, every aspect of human life would be unduly affected. The world will be in a state of panic for it will seem as though the world is shutting down before their very eyes. Yet, those who listen to the Father will understand what is taking place.

When technology becomes available again many will readily accept whatever transpires in hopes of regaining what they once had. That for them was their reality! The enemy will have used this time of darkness to implement the next stage of his **extreme plan**.

Since the inception of the *Corona Virus,* the division amongst the nation has slowly increased. The line is slowly but surely being drawn in the sand. There were now two opposing forces which were becoming increasingly apparent, that being *good versus evil*. This division is rapidly spreading throughout the world.

As a result of this division and upheaval, many will be seeking a peace that is nonexistent. Jesus warned Wendy and Jillian that when technology was up and running again there would be evil unknowns hidden within the system. A system that will not only track each and every being, but will be used to subliminally effect the minds of those who become enthralled with technology. ***This is the chip or mark of the beast which man had often referred to over the years.***

Jesus is protecting His chosen people. He also knew time was of the essence as the younger generations were now addicted to technology. Social Networks controlled the minds of the younger population and would severely alter, if not change, the moral compass of many generations to come.

Much the same as Satan had used the *Corona Virus* in his "**extreme plan**", for the fall of humanity, Jesus would allow the *Corona Virus* as part of His "**Supreme Plan**". He would use this time to separate the wheat from the chaff. This would be a time of trial that would eliminate those worldly distractions, thereby allowing more time for each to draw closer to their Heavenly Father. A time in which one could reflect on what was truly important in life.

For some, this span of time would be life-altering indeed. While some families would be torn apart as a result of the choices one would make, others would develop a bond that had been sorely missing in the past. Many would now approach life from the inside out as the outside world had become one of unrest and dis-ease.

Just as the *Corona Virus* was a practice run for the Mighty Deceiver, it was used by Jesus to awaken His precious souls to that which was the reality. Yes, to awaken all to a magnitude of evil many had not deemed possible in the twenty first century; a deception that had been masterminded by non-other than Satan himself.

Those who did not partake of the vaccine were prompted by the Holy Spirit to not succumb to that which they intrinsically knew must be avoided at all costs. This was not an easy stand to take as many would not only lose their jobs as a result, but would be severely chastised by those who felt this was an irresponsible position to take. For those who revered the Father, stand they did, trusting in the still voice within. These were the souls who were connected to the Holy Spirit and demonstrated faith over fear. These were the individuals Jesus knew would play a most important role in preparing the way for His Kingdom to reign on earth. Although Jesus would use the *Corona Virus* as a wake-up call for His beloved children, many would in the future choose fear over faith paving the way for the Antichrist to gain control. A control which in the end would lead to a time of trial, such as never before known to the modern man. Not since the days of Noah and Lot would humanity experience such total and utter devastation.

St. Michael and his Warriors were on high alert now, having seen in the spirit world that which much of man did not acknowledge. Mortal man could not sense the ferocity of the battle which was now taking place in the spiritual realm. A battle that would soon become apparent throughout the world and that mankind was not prepared to face.

Technology would be used to deceive those who would be captivated by what had been artificially configured. A deception that would convince many that the so-called miraculous signs they were witnessing were of the Heavenly Father. Just the same as those who were duped during the *Corona Virus*, they would eagerly react to that which was orchestrated by the Mighty Deceiver.

Once the Mighty Deceiver had control of these precious souls, he then would be able to introduce the **"*One World Order*"**, which he had been planning since the very day he had been thrust from heaven. A plan which was hell bent on destroying the souls who understood that which was the reality; those Spiritual Beings who knew intrinsically they were one with the Father's Spirit, and who pledged allegiance to the one and only Supreme Being of the Universe.

For this reason, the Prophets, Earth Angels, Spiritual and Prayer Warriors were now joining forces with St. Michael and his Warring Angels. Additionally, there would be those souls who had signed up to partake in the tribulation who would fight in the flesh the forces of evil which controlled the world.

This pre-tribulation would be the time in which those who resided on earth would help prepare the way for our Father's Kingdom to reign on earth. Each must trust, as a Spiritual Being, in that which they were endowed with. They would withstand the forces of evil as they moved ever forward preparing the way for others to follow.

THE GREAT PLAN

CHAPTER 30
THE GREAT PLAN
AND THE RAPTURE

As *Earth Angels*, Wendy and Jillian understood they had been sent to share God's messages with the world. And now they were called to share the most important message of all. That which would share the **"Father's Great Plan"**. One that was written through the Holy Spirit. A book that would enlighten many to that which is of the mind of Christ.

They knew there would be many who would be questioning why the Father would allow such a time of trial to take place upon the earth? Many would say, *"He was not a merciful God"*, and posed the question man had been asking for many centuries, *"Why did God allow bad things to happen to good people?"*

Wendy and Jillian had heard this question on more than one occasion. Especially when it came to the young and those who were incapable of defending themselves. They could understand why this would be on the minds and hearts of many who were now being severely impacted by events orchestrated by evil. Yet, they knew Jesus had been trying to open the eyes of His children to that which was looming on the horizon.

The Bible had included the *Book of Revelation,* which would alert all to what would be transpiring throughout the world in the last days, as well as to that which would be taking place prior to His second coming. One must remember God's timing is very different than man's timing, and so it was for mankind, there would be many years in which they would anticipate His return. As the years passed by, mankind became disenchanted with Jesus' imminent return doubting this was a reality, but more-or-less a fable from long ago. And so, it was no wonder those who had been schooled in religion, over time, doubted this would occur in their lifetime. As a result, many lived for today giving little if no consideration of what tomorrow would bring. Many would no longer adhere to the Lord's Commandments as they too were now outdated and did not fit the current needs of the culture. The time had come where these Commandments were now adapted to suit the current culture. A culture that was dependent on the material world and all the enticements it had to offer.

What had once been considered morally wrong, now, was considered morally right. Satan had done a good job of fostering the *devil may care* attitude. As a result, man had adapted a carefree, relaxed, and often reckless outlook on life. An outlook in which one did not seem to worry about the potential consequences of their actions regarding not only self but those around them as well. For many it had become a dog-eat-dog society.

Too many were now driven by self and selfish interests, being more than willing to exploit others. As a result, many governments had become infested with those who were prepared to do the devil's handy work.

Satan, who ruled the earth, had now infiltrated every aspect of one's life introducing a new reality that did not include that of our Heavenly Father nor the Kingdom in which He could be found.

Jesus knew there would come a time such as this. A time when, for many, there would be a rude awakening. Time was now running out as the enemy was ramping up for what would be, for him, the world in which he would soon dominate. He would be without those who revered their Heavenly Father's will above all else.

Jesus knew there would be many who would fall prey to the trappings and lies of the *Antichrist*. These were the ones who had not formed a relationship with their Heavenly Father. These were the ones who had fallen away from the Godly principles they once knew to be true, and now had replaced the spiritual with all that would encompass the material world and all who ruled it.

Still, there were those who revered the teachings of their Heavenly Father who knew what was of Him and what the reality was. As Spiritual Beings they were able to access the mind of Christ, as together they were one in the same Spirit. Jesus had promised, prior to His return, those who were of one Spirit, those who magnified the Lord, would be removed from the earth prior to a trial in which those who were left behind would have to endure.

It was interesting that as *Earth Angels*, neither Wendy nor Jillian, while in the human condition, had paid too much attention to what was referred to as "**The Rapture**". Neither of them considered this to be unusual as they intrinsically knew that whatever was needed the Lord would provide. Never, did they consider such would not be the case!

Now that the time was drawing closer for Jesus' return there was a great deal of discussion and anticipation among Christians regarding the Rapture which was referred to in the Bible. The Rapture as described *in 1 Thessalonians 4:16–17* is the moment when believers, both deceased and living, are caught up to meet the Lord in the air. This event is often viewed as a sudden transformative experience where Christians are taken up from the Earth to be with Christ. It symbolizes the gathering of the faithful, a Divine rescue from impending tribulation, and the beginning of eternal fellowship with the Lord. The Rapture is characterized by its immediacy and profound hope that it offers to believers who anticipate being united with Christ without experiencing death.

The **Great Tribulation** is the "wrath to come" from which the believer is delivered by the Rapture (1 Thessalonians 1:9-10 The children of God, because they have kept the word of His patience, will be kept from the hour of trial).

If you are reading this and the Rapture has not yet taken place, well then, you do indeed have something to look forward to. There are different opinions of when the Rapture will occur. Some believe it will occur prior to the seven-year tribulation. Others believe it will occur halfway through the tribulation. Jesus will confirm a covenant He had formed with many and as such, will put an end to suffering. They will be raptured before the most intense period of trial. The Rapture will coincide with significant prophetic events, such as the rise of the Antichrist. The post tribulation view argues the Rapture will occur at the end of the seven-year tribulation coinciding with the second coming of Christ.

Regardless of when it does occur, isn't it wonderful we have the assurance that when all is said and done those who believe in the Father will be reunited with Jesus. Because there was such a controversy among man regarding the Rapture, Wendy knew if she went directly to the Father, regarding the Rapture, she could trust in what she would hear.

Jesus Answers About The Rapture

"For I tell you this just as the enemy is coming after My precious souls, I am preparing the way for My chosen to join Me. Yes, when things seem as though they are spinning out of control I will come as a thief in the night. I and I alone will not allow Satan to steal My beloved from Me. I will not allow you to be stolen from that which I have prepared for you. I have formed a covenant with thee that cannot be broken! I will raise you up on angel's wings. Do you see yourself as an angel or do you see yourself holding on to the wings of a dove? As a Spiritual Being you are of My Holy Spirit. Those of you who embrace your true reality will indeed soar with the eagles. Those who desire

Me above all else will join Me in the clouds and soar to new heights. You know who you are and have no need of the physical or material world. My chosen must direct all thoughts inward sharpening your spiritual senses so you will be ready when the time approaches. For too long man has looked at death as an end rather than when one dies unto "self". This then is the beginning of a new tomorrow. My Kingdom will reign on earth as it is in Heaven when all who reign on earth are one in My Spirit. Do not concern yourself about the flesh for it is of no use to you as a Spiritual Being. You who have endured much are now finding your way back home. For this is your true home and I will not give the enemy the satisfaction of coming against My chosen. You will be raised up in the last days to join forces with all who revere the Father. You must trust in Me as I trust in you and the inner knowing of which you possess. Nothing must take precedence over this inner knowing. You have mastered faith over fear therefore, you will soar with the eagles as you have acknowledged you are one with Me. There is a new dawn on the horizon therefore do not cling to the world. For this world will be forever changed. There must be a day of reckoning. When My chosen no longer remains on this Earth all will see the magnitude of evil of which many have contributed to. None is without blemish. None has not been soiled by the nature of the beast. I am scouring the Earth for My remnant church and yes, at the appropriate time I will come for My people. Those of you who know Me know I am a God of truth. You can trust in what you hear for I have always said you will have what you need when you need it. This is yes, a part of My Great Plan. I am showing you what must be released before you are raised up on the wings of a dove. I will indeed come for My people!" - Jesus

CHAPTER 31
PLANTING THE SEEDS

Many have heard of what Christians depicted as the final Apocalyptic battle, Armageddon. This would be the final battle between good and evil. This is a battle between what is of the spirit and that which is of the flesh. Until humanity fully understands the nature of this battle, they truly, cannot understand the nature of the beast.

The nature of Satan, the beast, as he is often referred to, is the extreme opposite of that which is of the spirit. In order to understand the nature of the beast, Satan, the Mighty Deceiver's existence must not be ignored, although, it has been by a vast majority of mankind. Those who might slightly entertain the idea of his existence, in-truth, doubt he is alive and active in the world today. The key weapon here is **doubt.**

In the beginning, it was the serpent who caused Eve to not trust in what God said would happen if they were to eat from the tree of the knowledge of good and evil. If they were to do so they would surely die. And so, it was doubt that caused Eve to partake of the forbidden fruit.

Doubt is ever present in the world today and will play a significant role in the end times. The serpent, upon entering the garden of Eden, sowed seeds deep within the bowels of the earth. These seeds, when fully ripened, would be used to plant seeds of doubt disavowing the existence of Jesus, God, and the Holy Spirit. When this crop reached full maturity, it would be used by those who held no affinity to God and would be the arms and legs of the Mighty Deceiver in the greatest battle ever known to mankind. A battle that would be referred to as the final battle between good and evil. Just as in any battle, Satan would, at the appropriate time introduce the **Antichrist; *a being who would be so cunning, so appealing many would willingly succumb to that which would cultivate a New World Order***. An order where he, Satan, would reign Supreme over God's precious souls. Souls that he, since the beginning of time, had been hell bent on destroying. Those who did not succumb to his **"One World Order"** would be destroyed. Although there would be some souls who would become enlightened to the wiles of Satan, there would be many who would face a time of trial that one would be hard pressed to overcome.

As in any battle, timing is the key. Satan, who was now entering upon the world stage, had infiltrated an army of unsuspecting souls who now doubted in that which had been foretold in the Bible, and as a result, doubted in the very existence of Satan as well. Yes, the seeds that had been planted well within the bowels of the earth would now come against the true nature of God's people who identified only with "self", and that which was of the physical; to that which is of the flesh.

At the same time Satan had been sowing his seeds deep within the earth, Jesus had been planting His seeds as well. These would be the seeds planted in Heaven, which at the appropriate time, would be harvested upon the earth. Having also been given the necessary time to come to maturity, they too would be the arms and legs of those enlisted in the Father's Supreme Army. An army that would understand, at the appropriate time, they too were Spiritual Beings possessing what Satan would never have, the human body. And so it was, of course, necessary for Satan and his legion of demons to operate through the physical bodies of mankind.

CHAPTER 32
THE ONE WORLD ORDER

What had been brewing for many years well beneath the radar of mankind would soon manifest throughout the world. This evil plan, when fully implemented, would introduce a *One World Order* that many would confuse with the <u>New World Order</u> which would become apparent when Jesus' Kingdom would reign upon the earth. The New World Order, which man now referred to, in essence, was a One World Order established by a group of international elites who would control governments and media organizations, with the goal of establishing a global harmony so strong and powerful it would control countries and the human race. This *One World Order* is a secret globalist agenda conspiring to rule the world through an authoritarian one world government, which would replace sovereign nations and include an all-encompassing propaganda whose ideology is of the <u>New World Order</u>. This world order has its roots so firmly planted it would take someone to appear on the World Stage who would be able to expose the magnitude of evil this *One World Order* hoped to achieve. A plan which much of mankind was unaware of.

Wendy had been trying for a few days to write what was of the Holy Spirit. She knew she was being directed to talk about the *One World Order* and was seeking guidance on what the Father desired for her to write in **"The Great Plan"**. She knew it must not be influenced by that which was of her conscious mind, and so it was, she would wait upon the Lord for the words He would desire to be written. She knew without a shadow of a doubt these were the times that would be prevalent prior to the *Antichrist* becoming visible for all to see. Watching what was emerging on the world stage, she could see a **New World Order** beginning to form. A world that would provide an opening for the *Antichrist* to make himself known. The uncomfortable feeling she was experiencing was the calm before the storm. *"Oh"*, she thought, *"Jesus cannot like what was transpiring between nations."* Jesus had warned money was the root of all evil.

While Donald Trump had been sent to expose the corruption and magnitude of evil, he must understand this battle will never be won in the flesh. She was seeing how materialism was creating barriers to what Jesus' Spirit was trying to impart. This was a battle that would require the mind of a *Spiritual Warrior* to stand strong against the wiles of the enemy. While Trump possessed the Spiritual Gift of Wisdom, he must understand his gifts and talents could and would be used against him by the adversary. Trump was more than familiar with the pitfalls of the ego as he had spent much of his life amassing his fortune, masterminded by that which was of his ego. The ego was what he would depend upon to amass his worldly fortune. Jesus knew Trump would be the best man for the job. For he and he alone understood those who were filled with self and selfish ambitions. Those who were the elite masterminds of the **One World Order** would establish a *One World Government* whose objective would include the destruction of the United States. While it was that Trump was able to expose the magnitude of evil within the Government of the United States, and various other organizations, he must understand the power of the Holy Spirit, less he would become impaired, much the same as operating with one hand tied behind his back.

To Jesus it was becoming more and more apparent that all focus was now being placed on the material via the sparring of tariffs and territorial acquisitions. Discernment would be tantamount in the weeks ahead. When the ego becomes a double edge sword, discernment could be lacking, which would create barriers to what the Holy Spirit was trying to impart. Just as in the *"The Art Of The Deal"*, Trump must discern when it was time to hold and when it was time to fold. Satan would use the ego to pit rivals against one another. Rivals who would engage in the practice of saber rattling, which was a very dangerous practice without the guidance of the Holy Spirit, and also if not careful, would pave the way for the **One World Order** to take control of the world. This was a crucial time that would require all who worked for the Heavenly Father to be on high alert. Jesus knew humility was the cornerstone on which Trump must now depend. He must be willing to humble himself before the Lord, waiting on Him for the answers to achieve that which would result in right resolution for all concerned.

Although Trump had publicly acknowledged Jesus had spared his life from the assassination attempt, he must recognize the chaos and confusion on which the enemy counted on. A chaos and confusion which was a direct result of too many irons in the fire at one time.

Trump knew time was of the essence. He must understand all works together in the Father's time and not by the schedule of man. The current sparring between China and Trump is now controlled by man's ego. When the ego is in control right resolution for all will never transpire. Wendy and Jillian knew wars and rumors of wars were always a result of man's self and selfish interests.

The world peace which Trump speaks of will never come to fruition when it is based on the material interests of a nation. And so it is, a deal is only made when there is something of a mutual and lasting benefit to the parties concerned.

Just as there are modern day prophets who work for the Lord in the twenty first century, there are prophets in whom the cabal or elite members of the One World Order look for guidance and instruction. One of their elite leaders had said," *AI had already seized control of human attention, taking over social networks and the media, thereby deciding what millions would see.*" He reminded all how Lenin and Mussolini started as newspaper editors and then became dictators. Additionally, he stressed today's editors have no names because they are not human. He also said, *"Due to AI, for the first time in history, it would be possible to annihilate privacy. Now it would be possible for authoritarian regimes to monitor their citizens around the clock."*

These elite claim humans invented the entire concept of God in order to answer the unknowable and accept these great fictions as truth. The WEF is for the emerging global elite. Elite members in this open society forum do not go to church in the traditional sense. They go to The Assembly of the Worship of Humanity. It is here they listen to their High Priest of Society who states, *"Mankind needs no God for man is God."* The WEF, rather than humbly petition God during times of drought, famine pandemics and wars, will now establish themselves as gods all over the world laughing at the concept of trusting in a Creator and obeying His laws.

THE GREAT PLAN

CHAPTER 33
THE REMNANT CHURCH

Those who understand they are Spiritual Beings will have successfully transitioned now from the physical condition in which their soul had set up temporary residence. Habits which were acquired, as a result of this physical condition, would be replaced with those that are of a Spiritual Being. These habits would be harmonious with all whose only desire would be to fulfill the will of their Heavenly Father. As a Spiritual Being those who resided on earth would remain until it was no longer beneficial for one to do so.

Those who had fully transitioned into their rightful heritage would now be called to operate on two fronts. One that would be prevalent throughout the earth, and yes, one which would be active in the spiritual realm as well. As a result, those who were on earth would soon exhibit those traits which are natural for a Spiritual Being. These traits would manifest in ways that those who held fast to the physical condition did not partake of.

Satan was well-aware of the Spiritual Beings who remained on earth to stand strong against the foothold of the enemy. These were the ones in which the seeds of the Father had been planted. The ones who were now fully equipped with the gifts they would need to prepare the way for Jesus' second coming. These were the ones who had fully transitioned into their natural state prepared to fight in ways in which mortal man could not. In ways which would prove to be far superior to that of the demons who served in Satan's legion. These Spiritual Beings who were one with the Spirit of Jesus, possessed a strength that Satan did not possess. They possessed an inner knowing that would enable them to be one with the mind of Christ. As such, they would intrinsically know what to do and when to do it, being confident, they possessed all that they would need to prepare the way for the second coming of Jesus Christ.

Wendy could see how those of considerable wealth would be shackled to those things of the world. The wealth they had acquired generated a false sense of superiority. A sense of superiority when joined with others, of like minds and spirits, would ensure all were not only reading from the same book but on the same page as well. They believed, because of their fame and fortune, their intellect was far superior to those who revered the teachings of Jesus and who followed a different book upon which they orchestrated their lives. Rather than follow the teachings of Jesus, those of the elite believed they were man's answer to humanity. They had the answer to all that one would face in a world dominated by technology. A technology, that in the hands of self-proclaimed elites, who considered themselves a superior race, could ultimately lead to the destruction of God's precious souls. Yes, those who answered to a Higher Power, to that of a self-appointed hierarchy.

In preparing **The Great Plan,** Jesus knew there would come a time when Christians would be considered not only nonessential but would be hard pressed to survive that which the One World Order would mandate for all of humanity. Those who did not conform would fear for their very lives as much of society would turn against all who revered the Father. Wendy understood the magnitude of what she and Jillian were being called to write as far too many in the year 2025 were unable to decipher the *Book of Revelation*, let alone display an interest in the bible. **She recalled how many times Jesus had said, *"If there were no computers, if there were no bibles, if there were no books what would man do?"***

Each understood how AI would be capable of deceiving, even what some would consider to be the staunchest Christians, that the Antichrist was the long-appointed Messiah. Signs and wonders in the sky could easily be created by technological innovation which were not explained as the *Book of Revelation* at this time did not exist. For this reason, **The Great Plan** needed to be written in a manner the current culture could and would understand. Additionally, mankind was now able to alter the very weather patterns throughout the world. And so it is that many of the signs which had been foretold would transpire prior to Jesus' second coming, would be used by Satan to rid the world of all who revered the Heavenly Father.

Those who inhabited the earth and were a part of Jesus' Supreme Army must respond as Spiritual Beings. These instincts, when fully operational, would provide a source of strength in which those who worked for Satan and his legion were not prepared for. The Holy Spirit would manifest in ways those of the elite, with all their worldly gadgets, would not be able to defeat.

The veil had been lifted for all who had eyes to see and ears to hear. This would enable them to embrace the reality. It was time Jesus' chosen understood not only who they were but what they were capable of in the Spirit.

While those who were active participants in **Satan's Extreme Plan** were well versed in the ways of the world, they did not possess what comes from within, that which no man could destroy. Just as when the Holy Spirit descended upon the Apostles the same would become apparent in these last days for God's chosen. What mankind would label as miraculous would now become apparent to those who crossed the path of Jesus' chosen. They would be infused with a supernatural energy that was of the Father. He had assured them they would have within all they would need when needed. They would intrinsically know what to do and when to do it. A knowing that those who did not revere the Father would not possess. Miracles would indeed abound, which could only come from the Divine.

The *Covid Virus* was used as a practice run by the enemy to see how easily mankind could be controlled by fear. Those who trusted in our Heavenly Father did not take a vaccine that had not been adequately tested. Just as the enemy had used this as a practice run for what was to come, Jesus had used it as a practice run for His chosen. These would be the ones to help prepare the way for the Father's Kingdom to reign on earth, and would be able to withstand what much of humanity would succumb to. This would require that they would have access to what man would label as a *supernatural power,* but would be natural for those who responded as Spiritual Beings.

CHAPTER 34
THE SPIRIT IS WILLING
BUT THE FLESH IS WEAK

Wendy prayed with all her heart the words she would write would be exactly as the Holy Spirit dictated. Both Wendy and Jillian, having experienced the human condition, were well aware of the many temptations man would succumb to. Temptations that would direct one's attention to worldly things versus that which they would experience through the five senses of a physical being. As a result, a vast majority of humans approached life from the outside in, while relatively few approached life from the inside out.

Wendy and Jillian understood the magnitude of the Holy Spirit and what one was capable of once they understood they were Spiritual Beings. Having worked for Jesus, they loved and adored Him in many ways, which most humans on earth did not experience. "*Oh*", Wendy thought "*how mankind was missing out on a revelation that would dramatically change the way in which one approached their time on earth. Far too many humans were unable to experience that which had always been available to all who accepted Jesus Christ as their LORD and SAVIOR."*

Easter week was a most solemn and sacred time for a vast majority of mankind. Although many celebrated Easter for a variety of reasons few understood the full magnitude of Holy Week. No one except for those who walked through the seven days with Jesus could possibly understand what the disciples and those who revered Jesus felt. Those who loved Jesus would be hard pressed to believe what they were seeing and experiencing with their mortal eyes. Here was their beloved friend and mentor whose body had been ravaged beyond belief. Every wound was as though it had pierced the very heart of each disciple. They could only see through the eyes and emotions afforded a human being, which opened the door for doubt and fear to enter. As a result, she could understand how the disciples would start to doubt the supernatural power, which they had previously seen in Jesus. Wendy knew that once doubt entered into the mind of man it would open the door for fear to dominate one's thoughts and actions, causing one to react in ways they never thought they were capable of. Wendy recalled how

Jesus, upon entering the garden of Gethsemane, asked His beloved disciples to watch over Him for an hour while He prayed only to discover upon His return, they had fallen asleep. Upon awakening, the disciples were ashamed they had fallen asleep. *Jesus then explained how the spirit was willing and the flesh was weak.* Little did they understand the full magnitude of what was about to happen and what they would witness. At a human level they understood some of what Jesus had been preparing them for, but when it came down to the flesh, and their human emotions, they did not respond to what they felt in the spirit; that which they felt in their hearts.

Satan knew doubt would enter the minds of the disciples as they could not understand why Jesus would allow such a thing to happen. Wendy and Jillian, having experienced what the mind of a human could or could not comprehend, they as Earth Angels, knew the full magnitude of the Holy Spirit. They knew without the indwelling of the Holy Spirit man would be hard pressed to trust in what their beloved Jesus had taught the disciples over the past three and a half years. **Just as in the case of doubt and fear, faith**

without trust would not be able to withstand the ultimate trials and tribulations man would face, prior to the return of their beloved Jesus.

"Oh", Wendy thought, *"if man could only understand the importance of the Holy Spirit within. For it was through the Holy Spirit one would be given the spiritual eyes and ears to see that which was the reality. If only man knew where to find this Kingdom that somehow had eluded those who would now experience what was referred to as the tribulation. A time of trial which would transpire prior to the return of Jesus Christ on earth. Without the Holy Spirit one would not have the strength in which they would need to resist that which was of the Antichrist. That which would be the the most crucial decision one's soul could ever make."*

Wendy and Jillian knew time was of the essence. They knew this was the time they were sent for. They must help all understand what was required for the Holy Spirit to dwell within. She recalled the forty days in which Jesus appeared before the disciples to teach and prepare them for what they would need to go out amongst men and teach about their beloved Father.

Jesus taught the disciples about the Kingdom of God and where one could find such a Kingdom. He also spoke about the return of Christ in which He would rule as the King of Kings in the Kingdom of God, as His Kingdom would rule on earth as it was in Heaven upon His return. He taught them not to worry over material possessions and to share with those in need.

Wendy also knew there would be those on earth in current times who would be granted authority over evil spirits and diseases. That which was prevalent 2000 years ago would be magnified again in the twenty first century. Jesus taught the disciples about the Holy Spirit's role in their lives and the ministry He was entrusting them with. He made it clear the Holy Spirit would empower them to be witnesses and to fulfill His commission.

Just the same as the disciples were commissioned by Jesus to spread the message of salvation, there were currently those who were commissioned by the Father to accomplish various assignments. Those who had signed a covenant with Jesus prior to their arrival on earth. Yes, a binding agreement or promise between

God and humans. That is a most sacred and enduring relationship.

Wendy and Jillian knew the Kingdom of God could be found within all who accepted Jesus and would result in the Holy Spirit residing within. Those on earth who experienced the effects of a relationship with the Holy Spirit knew there was nothing like this to compare to that which was of mortal man and the conscious mind of which he was most familiar with. Without the Holy Spirit dwelling within, man would not find the strength to overcome the evil , that now was magnified throughout the world. The true believers would be filled with the power of the Holy Spirit. A power like non-other on earth!

"Please Jesus", Wendy begged, *"give Jillian and I the words to write in this most important book!"*. They had been commissioned to teach about "joy" and the Holy Spirit. Each knew how crucial it would be for all who resided on earth prior to Jesus' return.

Now, more than ever, all must understand that which is the reality. Jesus was not just a character in some fable. All must understand the reality of Jesus and Satan as well.

Wendy and Jillian knew the clock was ticking and time was of the essence. They prayed for protection against the wiles of Satan and the evil he was so famous for. Each knew that once doubt crept in, it would not be long before fear would follow in its footsteps. Once that transpired, one could be unduly detained from moving forward with what they were called to complete.

Wendy understood full well what the disciples faced as they stood by and watched their beloved Jesus incur the wrath of Satan. Mankind must understand Jesus' crucifixion was not simply the fable that Satan tried to impress upon the minds of the current generations. What Jesus represented and incurred is indeed the reality. Most important, all must understand that without Jesus, without His Spirit dwelling within, they would not be prepared for Jesus' return to earth.

Over 2000 years have passed and the writings of these beloved disciples are still being read throughout the world. These ordinary men that many considered to be undesirables, would become extraordinary in every way. In the beginning when Jesus gathered His disciples they came from various backgrounds and status. To say that each was a work in progress would be an understatement.

The disciples would learn how the ego and those traits the religious leaders were sorely lacking in would come to be known as the **Fruits of the Spirit** *(love, joy, peace, patience, kindness, goodness, faithfulness, gentleness, and self-control).* The intense love the disciples had for Jesus was based on those traits the government and those of religious authority did not possess. One would say, the traits of which they displayed were often judgmental, cruel, and self serving.

Can you imagine how wonderful it would have been to be in the presence of someone who was indeed the opposite of that which they had witnessed in the world? Both Wendy and Jillian, knowing Jesus the way they did, knew human beings could not possibly begin to understand the magnitude of the Father's unconditional love. Jesus often stressed, **"What was freely received should be freely given unto one another.**

Now is the time for all to understand that which is the reality. I am preparing My people for what is to come. The world in which My people reside is but a temporary condition in which your soul has resided. I am removing the veil so all can see that which is looming on the horizon.

You must all get your spiritual houses in order for the world as you have known it will soon pass away. Those of you who reside on earth in these times have chosen to be here. And so, it is you must understand what your destiny is and in doing so what is required of each of you.

Although your tasks and that which you are called to do may be different from one another, I have gathered you all together for each of you has a role to play. Each of you will serve according to your purpose and yes, according to My timing.

I have said there would be signs which would alert you that My return is drawing close. All one need do is look around and they will see that which I am alerting them to. Yes, many have been called and in the end few will be chosen.

This will be through no fault of My own for I have been preparing each of you for what is to come. Yet, there will be those who will be lost along the way but just as in the story of the Prodigal Son it does not matter who comes first or who comes last as in the end it simply matters that they come!" -Jesus

CHAPTER 35

THE BIRTH PAINS HAVE BEGUN!

The time of trials had begun! Wendy and Jillian could see the birth pains that were now manifesting throughout the world. Birth pains, which were rapidly increasing. *The Book of Revelation,* written well over 2000 years ago, specified that prior to Jesus' return, there would be a seven-year period like none other experienced upon earth. He warned there would be signs at the end where there would be widespread conflict and unrest among Nations. As a result, there would be wars and rumors of wars looming upon the horizon. The Bible foretold of widespread food shortages and outbreaks of disease. There would be earthquakes appearing in various places as well as unusual signs in the Heavens. Christians would be persecuted and targeted for their faith. Moral decay will become ever present, and as such, an increasing disregard for God's laws would transpire. The Bible warns the love of many will grow cold as people turn away from God. As a result, man will be more concerned with his own desires and pleasures than with spiritual matters. *The Bible warns of the appearance of a powerful and deceptive figure who will oppose Christ. The Antichrist will require the mark of the beast be received on the forehead or right hand with the number 666 as a symbol of allegiance to the beast. Without this mark no one will be able to buy or sell those things that were necessary to survive in the world of which they had become accustomed to.*

Although Jesus had said, *"No man may know the hour of My return."* He had said there would be signs that would be ever-increasing prior to His return to earth. Which brings us to where we currently are in July of the year 2025.

Wendy and Jillian, as Spiritual Beings, understood the meaning of the times in which they were living. All those who worked for the Father possessed an inner knowing that afforded them a heightened awareness of which mortal man did not avail himself of. When Jesus said," *No MAN will know the hour of My return."* He knew those who understood they were Spiritual Beings would be well prepared for what was to come. These were the ones who would hear what the Spirit was saying and see what was before them.

Much the same as when the disciples became imbued with the Holy Spirit, it would now be the same for all who revered the Father in the year 2025. For months Jesus had been stating the importance of His precious souls fully transitioning into that which was of their true nature, that of a Spiritual Being.

These were the ones who embraced the reality of who they were, and as such, remembered from where they had come. Each intrinsically knew what role they would play in these last days. Each understood they would play an integral role in what would become known as **The Greatest Plan ever known in the history of mankind**. The role each would play would not only help prepare the way for the Father's Kingdom to reign on earth, but would help play an active role in the Father's Supreme Army. An army, that in the end would destroy the evil which had spread its evil tentacles throughout the world.

All who worked for the Father were on high alert and must maintain an offensive posture at all times, less they be taken off guard. Jesus, as the Commander-

In-Chief of His Supreme Army, was well versed in the weapon's Satan would now hurl at His chosen. All must maintain a Warrior's stance at all times and be ready to act at a moment's notice. For this reason, it was crucial all pay attention to that which was the reality. That which lies beneath the surface, and in doing so, they would not fall prey to the wiles of the Mighty Deceiver. Jesus, as the Ambassador of Truth acting as Commander-In-Chief of His Supreme Army, would alert all to that which was forth coming.

The Mighty Deceiver, of course, had now implemented many facets of his **Extreme Plan** throughout the world. A plan that had been strategically executed throughout government factions. A group within a government dissenting from the opinions and interests of the larger group. A group and or groups, which would now infiltrate almost every aspect of society. As a result, under the guise of government, they would succeed in infiltrating the minds of the young introducing educational programs that would unduly effect morality to such a degree that right from wrong could no longer be differentiated, as wrong from right was now an acceptable part of the norm.

Religion was no longer looked at as a spiritual foundation, but rather one that no longer played an integral role in one's moral and spiritual development. Antisemitism runs rampant among colleges encouraging free speech, which incites hate and division, fueled on bias and lack of knowledge, yet non the less, a cancer if not controlled.

The United States Government had become a hot bed of deceit and evil agendas that if not put in check would not only destroy America it would destroy the World at large. If not put in check that which no one thought would transpire, as in the days of Hitler, could indeed infect the well-being of all humanity,

One would be hard pressed to acknowledge there was such a faction entitled "**The World Economic Forum**" (WEF), who's mission was to engage business, political, academic, and other leaders of society to shape global, regional, and industrial agendas. They aimed to improve the state of the world through public and private cooperation.

"*Omg*", thought Wendy, "*now I know why Jesus told Jillian and I to look beneath the surface!*" In researching the names of those who were in charge of the WEF, it became increasingly apparent those whom much of society had trusted or at the very least indifferent to, were actively planning for what would create a **One World Government**. This would give control to those who had amassed the largest fortunes throughout the world.

The plan which had been developed by these hierarchy's was now being implemented in ways most could not conceive possible. These individuals saw themselves as the elite, and as a result superior to much of mankind. Through this One World Order they would gain control of every social, physical and economic facet throughout the world. Those who did not readily accept the terms and conditions presented would be eliminated and disregarded as unacceptable members of society. Without the approval of the WEF many would, in the end, be hard pressed to survive.

The birth pains had become ever increasing since the beginning of 2025. Just in the United States alone there had been strange sightings of unidentified objects hovering in the sky over various states in the country. Eventually, these objects were identified as drones of which there was much discussion as to who and what was the cause. The attention would then shift to an intense fog that generated much chaos and confusion, as many tried to speculate on the particles that appeared within the fog. Not only did the fog keep one from seeing what was in the midst, it also provided a distraction from the drones.

Shortly, after the fog emerged, there was a bombing on Bourbon Street and a subsequent bombing, thereafter in Las Vegas. Both of which were set off by military elites for which there did not appear to be any logical explanation for. And in January 2025 a massive fire erupted in California, the likes of which has not been seen in many years.

Countries, which were once considered allies of the United States no longer considered themselves as such because of the tariffs that were being imposed nation by nation. Not every nation was interested in making a deal, and as such, new lines were being drawn in the sand. The scales were now becoming increasingly unbalanced as far more emphasis was now being placed on the almighty dollar rather than on the spiritual.

For this reason alone, Wendy and Jillian were becoming unduly alarmed. They knew full well one cannot serve two masters. Jesus had warned of the times mankind would find himself in. He, the Father, would make certain mankind understood that He was in charge and would not bless that which incites division and unrest.

Never had Wendy or Jillian seen so much division throughout the world. Division that was now being fueled by hatred and an evil anger which one would be hard pressed to extinguish.

Satan would use fear as a weapon that would render many unable to stand strong against the ego of those whose agendas were of self and selfish interests. Yes, that which was not in the best and highest interest of all concerned. She thought of the expression, "*being tossed around*", regarding making a deal, and now wondered how many were truly ready to make a deal with Jesus!

Wars and rumors of war were escalating at a feverish pitch. Peace agreements were being bantered about, only to be undone at the slightest provocation. Israel was currently involved in the war against Hamas while at the same time rumors of war are escalating between Iran and the United States. The war in the Ukraine continued as conflicts persist with Russia. Currently, the United States was militarily engaged with the Houthis.

"Half-truths" were the norm, as much was hidden beneath the surface in an effort to convince one all was going according to plan. Yet, truth, was now a commodity as the media was controlled by the elites, and so what was reported was often altered if not reported at all.

Artificial Intelligence was advancing at a rate many would not have believed humanly possible. It was becoming increasingly apparent that what would be used for good could, if in the wrong hands, perpetuate an evil of which man could face in the not-too-distant future.

To sum it up, these were uncertain times for the world! The United States, once viewed as the most powerful Nation on earth, was now desperately trying to undo the damage and corruption which had been strategically infiltrated throughout the United States over the past decade. Strategies which now must be destroyed as time was of the essence.

"WOW!", thought Wendy," if these were not birth pains of what was looming on the horizon one must be turning a blind eye to what was transpiring throughout the world." One Nation under God was desperately trying to restore a nation that once was founded on Godly Principles. Principles which had been altered to fit the current demands of the culture. A culture that no longer represented what had been agreed upon by the founding Fathers of the United States. In fact, the name United no longer applied, as much division and unrest remained ever present within.

This division ran far deeper than what most of humanity could comprehend. This division was of the Spirit. Two opposing forces of which much of mankind did not acknowledge. Jesus knew there would come a time when man would finally come face to face with the real enemy. Face to face with a force that was driven by none other than Satan, himself. Satan, having no body himself, would use the physical bodies of those who would keep man from understanding he was much more than the physical body he inhabited. Yes, that man was a Spiritual Being who possessed an inner power which had, up until now, not been proven to be a staunch adversary.

Jesus' timing was precise, and as such, had awakened all to what was the reality. No longer were Jesus' precious souls held hostage by that which was of the world, as they understood without any doubt, they were Spiritual Beings endowed with a *power* that would stand strong against the forces of evil. This was a mighty opponent that the Mighty Deceiver did not anticipate. An opponent who was led by Almighty God, an Army of Superior strength capable of fighting against the spiritual forces throughout the universe. This army would join forces with those who resided on earth and those who resided in the heavens above. Soon the trumpet would sound, and all would stand ready for the final battle between good and evil!

THE GREAT PLAN

CHAPTER 36
THE TRUMPET SOUNDS

All in the heavens were on high alert as well as those who resided on earth. Those in Jesus' Supreme Army were called upon to always maintain an offensive posture. They must be ready to spring into action at a moment's notice. Although the battle had been raging for quite some time in the heavens, the enemy was advancing on earth at a rapid rate.

On Earth, the Pope had recently passed away causing quite a stir in the religious communities, generating a great deal of chaos and confusion among the masses. Satan, would use this as an opportune time to incite doubt even in the most stoical of the religious, and as Saint Michael knew, once doubt appeared on the scene it was not long before fear would follow. Once fear took over the enemy would strike a mighty blow. Those who were now overridden with fear would become like putty in the hands of Satan, and the many demons who were ready to spring into action at a moment's notice.

There, of course, had been many recent events on earth that the Lord said would be present prior to His return. Those who were paying attention understood the meaning of the recent signs, and now, with the sound of the trumpet, understood they were being warned of what was soon to come.

As in Revelation, the sound of the trumpet was always heard before a major occurrence or event. Wendy and Jillian, being Spiritual Beings, did not doubt what the sound of the trumpet meant, nor were they in fear of what was to come. All *Earth Angels* must not become distracted by those who were unable to hear what the Spirit was saying. For as *Earth Angels* they must be able to hear and see what those of deaf ears and blind eyes could not see.

Now would be the time for all who worked for the Heavenly Father to make their presence felt in the spiritual realm, as well as to those on earth, who were in grave danger from what was soon to enter upon the world stage.

There were many Christians, who once the *Antichrist* appeared on the scene, would just as Peter did, deny they knew or had an affinity to Jesus Christ.

Worse yet, many would be deceived mistaking the *Antichrist* for their beloved Messiah. As in any plan, timing was crucial. If one were to move too soon it would not produce the desired results.

They knew the weapons that Satan would use against Jesus' precious souls, Jesus would use to His Supreme advantage. Every soul who worked for the Father would now implement those skills they had been prepared for. All would fulfill what they were destined to complete. These were the ones who had fully transitioned into the true nature of a Spiritual Being. Together, they would present a formidable force against the weapons of the enemy.

Jesus was cautioning His chosen to exercise discernment in all that was transpiring throughout the world. One, therefore, must be ready to respond to Jesus who, as the Ambassador of Truth, would speak to those who must act upon what His Spirit was alerting them to.

While there would be much division throughout the world, Jesus' chosen would come together in unison and harmony. All who worked for the Father would be one with the mind of Christ. As together they would be one in His Spirit. *"He that is in Me is far greater than He that is of the world".* And so it was, Wendy and Jillian understood what Jesus meant when He said, *"They would have what they would need as they needed it."*

Soon, very soon, His Spirit would be ever present in the work they would be called to do. Wendy fully understood why Jesus had asked her to focus so intently on the forty days in which Jesus appeared to the disciples, prior to what would come to be known as **"Pentecost"** throughout the religious community.

These forty days for the disciples would be used to complete the training they would need to spread the gospel of Jesus Christ throughout the world. They were being prepared to spread the good news about Jesus Christ and His role in God's plan for humanity's salvation. They would share the message that *"God had provided a way for humanity to be restored to Him through the sacrifice of his son, Jesus Christ, and that this message brings hope and the possibility of eternal life to all who believe".*

The disciples had spent three and a half years with Jesus as He walked the earth. Now they would learn and experience, firsthand, the magnitude of the Holy Spirit. Each disciple would come to understand and embrace *"He that is in Me is far greater than He that is of the world."* Jesus had told them," *It is far better that I leave so another can take My place." And so it was in the next forty days they would experience, in the flesh, that which He was speaking of.*

In the forty days between the resurrection and ascension He would teach the disciples about the Kingdom of God. He would provide them with infallible proofs that He was indeed alive. This period involved multiple appearances to the disciples reinforcing His message and preparing them for future roles. The Holy Spirit would now become infused within the disciples, which would enable them to perform the many miracles Jesus performed during His time on earth. The disciples did indeed, now, have within all they needed as they needed it!

Now in the year 2025 all who worked for the Heavenly Father would experience the power of the Holy Spirit in ways they had not experienced before. Wendy and Jillian knew that those who were called to prepare the way for the Father's Kingdom would in many ways, experience what the disciples had experienced prior to Jesus' final ascension.

Each, having seen Jesus in the flesh in years past, knew full well the reality of what many had yet to experience on earth. Each understood the current times, in many ways, were of major significance in July of 2025.

The Pope's recent passing and the recent retirement of Charles Kraus of the WEF would greatly impact future events throughout the world. Events that would determine the role Satan would play, as leadership roles would provide a window for the tribulation to enter unto the world stage!

Those who had not been paying attention to the signs of the time would be deceived by that which would come to be known as the "**One World Order**". Those who did not have the Holy Spirit dwelling within would suffer at the hands of those who held no affinity to God nor those who revered the Father.

As events unfold, more and more would be required of Jesus' chosen, yet they too would possess all they would need in the weeks ahead. Untold miracles would demonstrate to all the power of the Holy Spirit within those who would lead the way for others to follow!

One must remember, all that had been foretold in the *Book of Revelation* was never a matter of if, but was, however, a matter of when. Many had tried to predict the time of Jesus' return, but none had been able to ascertain, precisely, when that would be. Jesus had specified the events and signs that would transpire prior to the tribulation, a seven-year period in which the enemy would rule the world.

Those who were filled with the Holy Spirit, intrinsically, knew time was now running out for those who did not accept Jesus Christ as their Lord and Savior. Because there were many who did not have a relationship with the Heavenly Father, they would lack the ability to discern that which was the truth and that which was of the *Antichrist*.

By the time many understood the magnitude of what they were facing they would be under the control of an evil so great that without the help of Jesus they would suffer a fate that one could not begin to imagine.

Those who were filled with the Holy Spirit would be able to stand strong against the wiles of Satan and those who were of his persuasion.

Our **Father's Great Plan** would now unfold exactly as He had planned. His Remnant church would endure what was to come. This mighty Army would stand strong against the forces of evil. Jesus would never turn His back on His precious souls, yet it was up to each soul to make the most important decision one could or would ever make.

"It does not matter who comes first nor does it matter who comes last, it simply matters that you come!" -Jesus

PART 4

THE GREAT PLAN

CHAPTER 37
THE TRANSITION

Every soul who resides on earth in these last days understood the meaning of the times they now found themselves in. These times had been foretold well over 2000 years ago. Although most would not remember the time before they had inhabited the earth, every soul had been informed of what they would encounter. As a Citizen of Heaven each understood this was but a temporary residence in which they would reside.

Jesus had explained to every soul they would be subject to the *human condition,* which would create barriers to what every soul was trying to achieve. For each soul it could be different depending on that which was the sole purpose for his stay on earth. The soul understood he was a Spiritual Being, and as such, relied on the senses of a Spiritual Being.

All who resided in heaven were aware there would soon be a *new world* that would emerge as more and more souls were able to assume their rightful position in the physical body. A position, that for many, had been ignored by a vast majority of humans. Every soul had been created in the Father's image. An image that was perfect in every way. To evolve and become more proficient in the ways of the Heavenly Father each would need to have access to the mind of Christ. Jesus Christ had been sent by the Father to awaken man to the ways of the Divine. Therefore, it was imperative each soul be able to have access to what they knew was their right and true domain as a Spiritual Being. Now in the year 2025, there were many souls who had awoken as if from a deep sleep. The veil for many had lifted. The soul now understood not only from where it had come, but where it would return. Because each had enrolled in the School of Life on earth, they had experienced firsthand the many weapons Satan would use to keep man from understanding he was not the sum-total of the physical condition in which he found himself. He was a Spiritual Being who would, in the last days, stand strong against the forces of evil running rampant throughout the world.

These precious souls possessed an inner knowing that had been instilled in each soul prior to their arrival on earth. Every soul would be equipped with a *spiritual gift* that would assist them in what would be needed for them to accomplish their earthly mission. While the mission could be different depending on the task each would be called to complete, there would be a common goal. One that would ensure the enemy would be destroyed, paving the way for Jesus' Kingdom to reign on earth. Two such souls who resided on earth, currently, were none other than Wendy and Jillian. Their sole mission was to insure all had access to the mind of Christ. Mankind must understand it was the Holy Spirit who provided a direct link to the Heavenly Father. The Holy Spirit was the conduit to the Divine. Wendy and Jillian must help all to understand they were in fact Spiritual Beings. It is this reality that would enable each soul to transition to a higher state of being. It would be now that mankind, who currently found themselves in the third dimension, would make a shift into a far better dimension. To understand the essence of this dimensional shift, it is important to understand what the Third Dimension is and what it is not.

THE GREAT PLAN

CHAPTER 38
THE THIRD DIMENSION

The Third Dimension often refers to the physical and emotional aspects of human existence encompassing one's everyday experience and perception of reality. The key word here is *perception,* as it is not the reality man was created for. The Third Dimension represents one's familiar sense of "self", including physical awareness, emotional responses, and mental process. It is the space where man develops his personality, thoughts, and emotions within the physical world. **Currently, earth is relegated to all that is of the Third Dimension**. Relegate, as webster defines: *to put into a lower or less than important position.* All that is relegated to the human condition includes the conscious mind. The conscious mind is how man understands that which is of the physical world with sights, sounds, smell, and sensations. As a result, man develops mental theories and attachments as he experiences the world through these senses. In the Third Dimension one perceives things in terms of opposites (*example; good and bad,*

234

right and wrong, win and lose, separation and competition).

There is a strong sense of ego and materialism. People in the Third Dimensional state are more concerned with personal gain and less concerned with unity. Satan, who dominates the Third Dimension, will use all that is of the world to limit man's capacity to go beyond what his senses experience in the flesh. Although the soul resides in the center of every human, very little attention in the Third Dimension is given to the soul who without this ability to connect to the Spirit of our living God will surely loose its way. Because there are so many distractions to occupy man's mind, he approaches life based on that which is of the exterior, the material or physical.

The Lord has now lifted the veil, and as a result, those who are listening will embrace they are in fact, Spiritual Beings. In order for His Kingdom to reign on earth, it is necessary one exercise a higher consciousness being aware of an existence far superior to that of the Third Dimension.

CHAPTER 39
THE FOURTH DIMENSION

In the Fourth Dimension spiritual concepts extend beyond the Third Dimension exhibiting a higher level of consciousness, intuition, and spiritual awareness. A Spiritual Being can perceive time more fluidly and experience an interconnectedness to higher frequencies. Spiritual Beings will assist our Father in raising the earth's dimension to that which exemplifies the Kingdom of God.

The heightened awareness of the Spiritual Being understands the importance of destroying the evil which is ever prevalent in the Third Dimension. Together, with like-minded spirits, a new energy will surpass that which is of the Third Dimension. There is a greater sense of interconnectedness with all things where one can connect with higher beings and energy. Individuals have heightened intuition, clairvoyance and a greater capacity for empathy, and often associate with spiritual realms, such as the Kingdom of God where individuals can connect with higher beings and energies.

In the Fourth Dimension there is a higher consciousness which enables one to connect with the mind of Christ. Those thoughts and ideals which are of His Spirit.

In the Third Dimension those who restrict their thinking to that which is of the conscious or physical have lost their ability to embrace that which is of their true, identity. A Spiritual Being understands the nature of the BEAST which in the Third Dimension dominates the nature of man.

The Fourth Dimension is something God wants the whole world to see. When Christ returns He will change the world. The chosen ones are being prepared for this dimensional shift embracing the mission each is called to fulfill. As a result, a new world is indeed coming as this heightened awareness will manifest in ways commensurate with that of our Father's Spirit. A dimension that will prepare the way for His return.

HEAVEN

I awoke this morning in a strange kind of place, Why oh why does everyone walk around with such a smile on their face?

The streets are all paved in silver and gold, while here it appears no one grows old.

There are familiar faces it seems I should know. Perhaps they are faces from long, long ago?

There is a such peacefulness here I can't quite understand, it seems to be present throughout much of this land.

The meadows how they sparkle all covered in dew, everywhere one looks there is such a spectacular view.

238

I feel at home in this place, it is as though I have returned. From where I ask and what have I learned?

You have come from the School of Life, a passerby volunteers. Do not be alarmed for you do belong here.

You have successfully completed the Pathway to the Divine, but as you are discovering this is not the end of the line.

You will learn much here if you but stay the course. For in Heaven you will find there is no remorse.

Do I want to Go Back? I really can't say. Maybe I will just think on it for one more day!"

ABBA and Company

CHAPTER 40
SATAN AND THE CONSCIOUS MIND

Satan avails himself of the conscious mind of mankind using all that is available to ensure man's mind is preoccupied with self and all that is of the exterior. Webster defines conscious mind as: *the mind that is aware of one's thoughts feelings, memories, and the external world at any given moment.* Satan knew that as long as he could keep mankind entrenched in the Third Dimension, all would be subject to the human condition which included, first and foremost, the conscious mind. If man directed his full attention to self and selfish ambitions, he knew unity and harmony would be non-existent in the last days. He knew the conscious mind would draw conclusions based on outside stimuli and the five senses afforded man's physical self. While these five senses are necessary to function on earth, they are of no use to a Spiritual Being.

This is what man understood to be a human being. This is, of course, the greatest deception of all time.

240

Webster defines being: *as something that is conceivable and capable of existing.* In short, the physical self was designed solely to exist on earth. Satan, who dominates the Third Dimension, uses all that is of the world to limit man's capacity to go well beyond the five senses experienced in the flesh. Although the soul resides in the center of each human, little attention is given to the soul, who without the ability to connect to the Spirit of our living God, will surely lose his way. Because there are currently many distractions to occupy the mind of man, he approaches life based on all that is of the exterior. All that is of the material world in which he inhabits.

When one understands the magnitude of the Third Dimension and how it operates, one can fully appreciate why *Earth Angels* were now scattered throughout the world and would play a major role in the **Father's Great Plan**. Together, with like minds and kindred spirits, they would help prepare the way for the Father's Kingdom to reign on earth. The Third Dimension embodies the physical and emotional aspects of human existence that encompasses one's everyday experience and perception of reality. The

Third Dimension is representative of "self", which includes emotional responses to outside stimuli and mental process.

THE GREAT PLAN

CHAPTER 41

THE HIGHER CONSCIOUSNESS

As *Earth Angels,* Wendy and Jillian understood the necessity of exercising one's higher consciousness, fully aware of an existence far superior to that of the Third Dimension. For months, the Holy Spirit had been stressing the importance of His beloved souls transitioning from the physical to the true nature of a Spiritual Being. This transition would prove to play a major role in preparing the way for the Father's Kingdom to reign on earth.

Those who were unable to exercise their higher consciousness would not be able to survive the trials mankind would soon be facing. The ability to exercise one's higher consciousness as a Spiritual Being would be their saving grace in the end. This ability would not only prepare them for what was to come, but would ensure they did not fall prey to the weapons the Mighty Deceiver would use against God's precious souls.

It is crucial one understands Satan uses a conscious mind to control how man reacts to the world. Often, conclusions are based on what one perceives to be true. The thoughts of the conscious mind are much like a magnet. These thoughts become ingrained, making it impossible to see what is the reality. These thoughts then become part of the subconscious mind. Webster defines the subconscious as: *the part of the mind in which one is not fully aware, but what influences one's actions and feelings.* As a result, reactions are based on human emotions that do not exemplify the traits of a Spiritual Being.

As a Spiritual Being, it is quite clear thoughts or one's higher consciousness are not of man's conscious or subconscious thoughts. For the mind of the Spiritual Being is directly connected to the mind of Christ and the senses which are afforded a Spiritual Being.

Wendy and Jillian remembered when they first experienced the human condition. What they experienced was based on internal stimuli; *an inner knowing which comes from within.* As time progressed, they became more and more affected by that which was of the exterior. They experienced firsthand how a child becomes increasingly affected by that of their environment. As a result, their beliefs and personality are based on the surroundings each found themselves in. Surroundings that were based on perception and not, reality. That which one perceives himself to be through the influences he is surrounded by.

Spiritual Beings are created in our Father's image, an image which is perfection and untarnished by mankind. Therefore, one's higher consciousness is directly related to the mind of Christ. It is far superior to man's conscious mind and the subconscious mind, which stores thoughts and feelings that create barriers to one's higher consciousness. *Earth Angels* knew, as Spiritual Beings, they would no longer gravitate to that which was of the conscious mind, rejecting all that created barriers to their true, identity. They knew gravity was a force that attracts the human body towards the center of the earth or any other physical body. Satan, as a result, uses the mind of a human to keep him preoccupied with that which is an illusion. As a result, much of mankind currently behaves according to what he believes to be true, not that which is the reality of a Spiritual Being.

THE GREAT PLAN

Jesus' timing is perfect. His timing is precise in ways man cannot begin to understand. Now in the year 2025 there were many signs which pointed to the tribulation. Times of trials, such as man had not experienced since the days of long ago. Although many were familiar with the stories in the Bible, such as Noah's Ark, Moses, and the parting of the Red Sea, far too many did not think anything of such magnitude would happen in the current century. In truth, a great many no longer believed in Jesus Christ let alone His second coming.

CHAPTER 42
THE CHOSEN ONES

If you are reading this book, never doubt, you are prepared for times such as these. Unlike many, you now know who to turn to, and where your strength comes from. When you approach all from the inside out, you can be assured our Father is in you and you are in Him. Together, you are one in His Spirit. He knows the measure of your heart, and as such, every thought you think. Our Father is not concerned about the random thoughts that come and go, but rather those thoughts that create barriers to your higher consciousness. When you doubt, you are being prodded by the enemy to dwell on that which mortal man defines as impossible or even undesirable.

You have at your disposal everything of our Father's Kingdom. The answers you receive are far superior to that which lacks Divine understanding. You will experience miracles. He will work through those whose hearts are pure. Simply, humble yourself before our Lord trusting He is in control. You are well seasoned, humbled by your own sins and failures, seeking after all that is of God.

In the days ahead, you will understand those who know, know! and those who don't, won't! You will be among those who look forward to the glory, and yet there will be those who will not be able to move through the darkness that is soon to come. This, for many, will be the dark night of the soul. Because you are one with our Father's Spirit, this darkness will not pervade your soul as His light will shine through for all to see.

Yes, my friend, you among others will be the candles in the darkness holding onto the wings of a dove. You will soar with the Eagles. There is a *New World* emerging that will glorify our Lord. A world in which you will surely play a part. Together, we will help prepare the way for our Father's return. Make ready, my friend, for the day of judgment is at hand, and so it is, all will see who is in control.

The enemy is advancing at a rapid rate, yet our Father is prepared for what is to come. Together, we must continue to move forward assured He is in us and we are in Him. You are meant for these times and are at a critical juncture; *a place at a critical point in time.*

We must all take up the shield of faith as we are protected by the breast plate of the Holy Spirit. We must humble ourselves before the Lord. Trust, therefore, in what you hear, obeying all that is of His will in these last days. These will not be the last days for His remnant church. There is a *New Dawn on the Horizon,* and so it is, you must understand it is always darkest before the dawn.

Our Father will use all things in all ways to His Supreme advantage. There will be many who will flounder helplessly, much like a fish out of water. They will react to the chaos and confusion, yet you, My chosen, will be made surefooted as our Father, the Commander-in-chief, leads us through troubled waters.

THE GREAT PLAN

CHAPTER 43
NEWFOUND AWARENESS

With your newfound awareness, you can observe with the senses of a Spiritual Being. Just as our Father knows the real you, when you see through the eyes of the Spirit you embrace there is a precious soul temporarily residing within every human. Every soul is here for a specific purpose. For each soul it can be different depending on what they have learned and what they desire to become proficient in. It is imperative that when you see someone struggling you reserve judgment, asking the Lord, how you can assist them as they struggle to move forward in their soulful education. As a Spiritual Being, you are endowed with an understanding, which will enable you to demonstrate the love of our Heavenly Father. You now possess a higher understanding of what lies beneath the surface in every being. When you remember all souls are here to *learn, to serve and to grow*, you will reserve passing judgment, which will only create a barrier to one's soulful development.

THE GREAT PLAN

As a Spiritual Being, you must not justify that which excuses us from assisting another soul as they struggle to overcome what their soul is desperately seeking. When you exercise your higher consciousness, you will respond to others as our Father responds to each of us. Wisdom therefore, is learned and as a compassionate being we too will struggle as we continue to exemplify the ideals of our Heavenly Father.

CHAPTER 44
HIGH ALERT

You will be experiencing an intensity now which is a sign your spirit is on high alert! Do not liken this intensity to one of dread. It is an awareness that supersedes that of the physical senses. Many times, lately, our Father has said, ***"Be still and know that I am God."*** It is in this stillness you must listen.

The enemy will try to use your conscious mind to interrupt what comes from within. Simply, acknowledge he is closing in and ignore the gravitational pull Satan is using to distract you from the Holy Spirit. You are a Spiritual Warrior and you are most familiar with the weapons he will try to use against you. You understand who you are and will automatically behave according to what you know to be true.

Those who stay close to our Father will see what others turn a blind eye to. Rejoice, for you are among His chosen in whom He is well pleased! Our Father assures us you will have what you need when you need it and will respond as our Father would respond, for you have within you all you need to do so. Trust in Him as our Father trusts in you. His Spirit will manifest for all to see. *"Help is on the way! You will see! You will hear! And yes, you will speak through me!"* says the Lord.

CHAPTER 45
THE GLORY

"The Glory of the Lord already exists within all who accept Jesus Christ as their Lord and Savior. When we look outside of ourselves for confirmation or manifestation of the Holy Spirit we neglect the reality. We have within all that is of the Holy Spirit. The special gifts and dispensation of the Holy Spirit are only restricted by that of the conscious mind. Therefore, he that believes in Me will see Me. He that believes in Me will hear Me. Together, We are one in My Spirit and so it is all that I have you have at your disposal.

When I spoke of the Fourth Dimension, it is a reality for those who revere the Holy Spirit. My Glory is of the Fourth Dimension and those traits associated are of the Father. These traits or characteristics are of the Father will come to pass and be ever present when Jesus returns to Earth. Therefore, it is a reality that the Third Dimension will shift into that which exists within the believers who are of My Remnant Church. Once again, I tell you. My Glory lies within all who have accepted Jesus Christ as their Lord and Savior and revere the Holy Spirit.

The more you seek, the more you will find. The more you find the more you will display. There can be no resistance and no room for doubt. When you doubt you will not behave according to that which is of My Glory. You will behave according to that which you have limited yourself to as a physical being. Therefore, go forth with this new understanding that as a Spiritual Being you have all you need as we transition from the Third Dimension to the Fourth Dimension. This is how you will help prepare the way for My Kingdom to reign on earth.

I alone know the measure of each of your hearts. I know what you are capable of through Me. I only ask you welcome Me with open arms, trusting in all I have planned for each of you. There is none on this earth who is *free of sin and so it is, I will empower you with that which will demonstrate the magnitude of My Spirit.*

Rejoice, for there is a new world on the horizon! A world in which we will all play a part. May God Bless and keep you safe as together we continue to pave the way for My Kingdom to reign on earth!" - Jesus

THE GREAT PLAN

CHAPTER 46
THE CONCLUSION

Wendy and Jillian prayed with every ounce of their being that whoever came upon this book would understand what was the reality of life and not that which was the illusion. All must understand not what is based on perception, but rather that which is God's honest truth!

Jesus had asked for them to divulge all that was of His plan from the very beginning of time. A plan that in the end would defeat the enemy. The battle between good and evil is a battle that has been fought since the beginning of time. A battle that has not nor would it ever be won in the flesh. It is a spiritual battle between principalities.

A PERSONAL NOTE TO THE READERS
FROM
WENDY AND JILLIAN,

"When you begin to understand the reality of who you truly are and what you are capable of in His Spirit it will open the door to a relationship like none other on this earth. You were created in our Father's image not in the image of man. You are beautifully and wonderfully made!

We have done our best with the guidance of the Holy Spirit to include all that will enable you to understand the reality. Your soul has chosen to be here in these times and as difficult as it may seem when you rid yourselves of those things which has kept you tied to the world and its many distractions, you will begin to acknowledge your beautiful soul within. Your soul knows who you are, where you have been and what your destiny is; that which you and you alone need to complete.

We have shown you what is necessary in order for the Holy Spirit to reside within. When you accept Jesus Christ as your Lord and Savior His Spirit will guide you through the troubled waters of tomorrow. There are many upon this earth, in these last days, who are here to assist you on your journey. There are those who will cross your path eager to light the way for you to follow. Our Father loves you more than words could ever express.

Do not lament over the past for what is done is done. Trust, therefore, in our

Heavenly Father as He trusts in you. Simply put one foot in front of the other as you absorb this newfound awareness. You will be given fresh eyes in which to view all that is around you and yes, the ears to hear what His Spirit is saying!

Hopefully, this book will come to you at the precise time in which you need it. There is much we have longed to share with the understanding this book must be completed in a timely manner. No matter where you are in the world or what is transpiring in your life God's timing is perfect and so it is your time to hear what His Spirit is saying.

This book is a gift to you from the Holy Spirit as we are only Earth Angels who have been sent to Earth in these times to share God's messages with the world. A message meant for you!

May God Bless and keep you in the days and weeks ahead. Together we will prepare the way for His return!"

Joyfully,

Wendy & Jillian

www.ingramcontent.com/pod-product-compliance
Lightning Source LLC
Chambersburg PA
CBHW071715120626
46550CB00001B/247